*Author Ivan Ponting and photographer Steve Hale are grateful to:*
*Ian Callaghan, Roger Hunt, Phil Thompson, David Johnson,*
*Alan Kennedy, Ronnie Moran, Roy Evans, Sammy Lee,*
*Tommy Smith, Ron Yeats, Eddie Marks, Steve Small, Stephen Kelly,*
*Les Gold, and Colin Hunt of the Liverpool Daily Post and Echo.*

*Published by:*
*The Bluecoat Press*
*Bluecoat Chambers*
*Liverpool L1 3BX*

*Design: Graham Nuttall*

*Origination: Almond Jones Merseyside Ltd.*

*Print: Printeska*

ISBN 1 872568 17 3

# THE BOOT ROOM
## An Anfield Legend

*Ivan Ponting*
*& Steve Hale*

**THE BLUECOAT PRESS**

# FOREWORD BY NESSIE SHANKLY

I am pleased to write a few words about this book, THE BOOT ROOM, because it gives me the chance to mention the people who worked so hard and so faithfully alongside my husband, Bill, at Anfield over the years.

Of course, the Boot Room was not a place that I visited. It was an inner sanctum for men only, and I was content to let it remain so. That's where they gathered together to plot and plan the future. I believe that much more was worked out in that little room than in the manager's office.

Bill thought a lot of the others, the likes of Bob Paisley, Reuben Bennett, Joe Fagan, Ronnie Moran and Roy Evans. They were good, honest men who knew their jobs and did them well. They were a real team, all pulling together for the benefit of the club, and Bill was proud of what they achieved.

Football was my husband's occupation and it took up most of his time, but I did not begrudge a minute of it. If he was happy, then so was I.

I never felt neglected, and there is no truth in the old story that he took me to a football match on our honeymoon. That was in June - he would never have got married during the football season. I must admit that there is just a grain of truth in the tale, though. One time he took me out on my birthday and we ended up across the Mersey watching Tranmere Rovers. That was a real treat!

We knew many marvellous times together and it gave me a lot of satisfaction that he was so successful. Of course, it wasn't always easy. When he arrived the club had been in the wilderness for a long time, but after a few years it all came together.

Football means so much to the people of Liverpool and it's good to feel that Bill is still loved today. It's truly wonderful that he hasn't been forgotten.

But the club has never been all about just one man, as this book makes clear by revealing much of what went on behind the scenes. THE BOOT ROOM will bring back a lot of treasured memories for the many thousands of people who have followed Liverpool over the last 30 or so years. It's a fascinating story; I think they'll enjoy it.

*Opposite: Behind every great man . . . Bill and Nessie Shankly after the Liverpool manager had collected the OBE in 1974.*

**The Boot Room was so workaday, so lacking in pretension,
so honest - just like, in the good years, Liverpool Football Club itself.
It was important not for what it was, but for what it stood.**

In the beginning there was Bill Shankly. Well, not literally the beginning - there had been a Liverpool Football Club since 1892, and it had known great moments, notably five League Championships in the first half of the century. But it was on that day in December 1959 when the inspirational, outrageous, all-consumingly enthusiastic little Scot stepped proudly across the threshold of Anfield as manager that a dozing, complacent, well-nigh comatose organisation was reborn as a soccer institution that would bestride the sporting world.

His predecessors in the hot seat, Don Welsh (1951-1956) and former team captain Phil Taylor (1956-1959), had been good men and true, giving their all to the task of guiding the club's fortunes, but they were not capable of sparking the Reds' renaissance. Shankly was different. He was a footballing evangelist with a vision. For Liverpool, he was the right man at the right time.

From his playing days with Preston North End and his managerial stint with Huddersfield Town, Bill knew all about Anfield and the state into which the Merseyside club had fallen. In later years he recalled an occasion in October 1958 when a ten-man Huddersfield had thrashed the Reds 5-0; though delighted at his own side's success, in a way the result saddened him. Another day he had watched the Reds humbled by an Everton team who, that brilliant schemer Bobby Collins apart, were nothing special themselves. The Blues' fans had mocked their wretched rivals and Bill Shankly had shaken his head in something close to despair.

Quite simply, he recognised that the Liverpool team was not worthy of the Liverpool people. They were proud, knowledgeable and soccer-mad. They reminded him of Glasgow and its folk, so gritty and passionate and humorous. They deserved a club which reflected their own devotion to the game, one which could capitalise on the vast potential they represented.

Instead they were stuck with one which seemed content to mark time in the upper reaches of the Second Division, enjoying minor triumphs but never challenging to be the best. This chronic lack of ambition and apparent absence of real self-esteem was reflected by a run-down ground that really didn't merit the grander title of stadium. Though partly due to the inescapable depredations of the war years, Anfield was tatty, second-rate and utterly unlikely to inspire pride of performance. Similarly the training headquarters, across the city at Melwood, was akin to a wilderness, with not a modern facility to be found.

When the call came in December 1959, Bill Shankly knew he had to go - his life's work was beckoning. He understood, felt with every fibre of his soul, the magnitude of what could be achieved with the raw materials to hand. As it turned out, they were even more bountiful than he might have imagined. Most new soccer bosses expect to recruit, or take with them, backroom staff to support their own fresh ideas. But when Bill reviewed the human resources available to him at Anfield, he was quick to realise that the bones of an outstanding off-the-field team were already in place.

A certain Bob Paisley was first-team trainer, with Reuben Bennett also on the scene as chief coach, and Joe Fagan was in charge of the reserves; Ronnie Moran, later to be such a colossal influence in the preparation of successive outstanding sides, was operating as an accomplished full-back, though it would not be long before his potential for inspiring others would be noted and he, too, would join the backroom brigade.

It was now that Bill laid down the creed that was to form the basis of the most successful long-term sequence any English football club has ever known, or is ever likely to know. Yet contrary to popular myth, there was no deep, dark secret or closely guarded formula. After all, if Shanks had been in possession of some magical blueprint for unlimited glory then he would

*Opposite:*
*The spoils of victory:*
*Bill Shankly and assorted*
*silverware in 1967, notably*
*the League Championship*
*trophy and the Charity*
*Shield. Behind him are the*
*men he once described as 'the*
*best football players you could*
*find on this earth.'*
*Left to right:*
*Ian St John, Ian Callaghan,*
*Roger Hunt, Gordon Milne,*
*Peter Thompson, Ron Yeats,*
*Chris Lawler, Tommy Smith,*
*Geoff Strong, Gerry Byrne,*
*Willie Stevenson and*
*Tommy Lawrence.*

*On parade in St Louis in the summer of 1964. This beaming sextet of Reds on tour comprises, left to right, Alf Arrowsmith, Ron Yeats, Ian Callaghan, Gerry Byrne, Ronnie Moran (later to become a Boot Room stalwart) and Ian St John.*

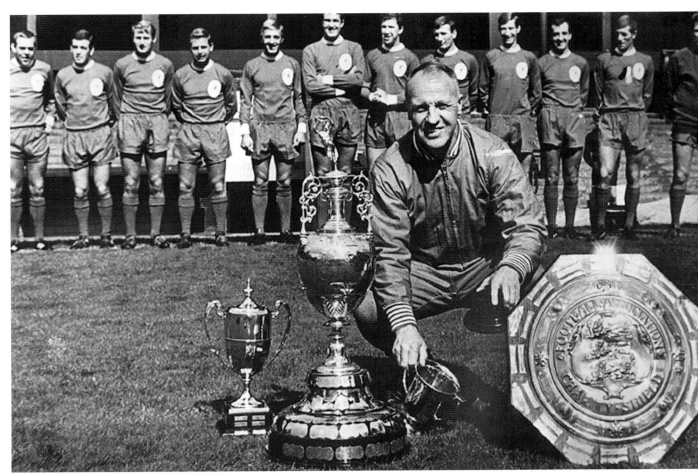

have employed it elsewhere, certainly at Huddersfield which was no small club. No, it was all much simpler than that.

He informed his lieutenants that he had his own training methods which he would explain to them so that before long they would all be on the same wavelength. Beyond that, he demanded loyalty: 'I don't want anybody to carry stories about anybody else . . . if anyone tells me a story about someone else, the man with the story will get the sack. I don't care if he has been here for 50 years.' He specified that everything they did would be to further the cause of Liverpool FC - an outlook that would make for strength.

Ronnie Moran recalls: 'He didn't come in wielding a big axe, but he made it plain that things would be done his way. He looked at what was good and he kept it. Then he added his own ideas. He liked everything to be simple, but later on, when people were looking for Liverpool's secret, not everybody could see the simple part.' Ronnie added that the support Bill requested was forthcoming unreservedly: 'Reuben, Bob and Joe were loyal men and they backed the manager to the hilt in every situation. That has gone on ever since, whoever the manager has been. It's the only way.'

Thus a dynasty was founded on loyalty, honesty and, it was to emerge over and over again, doing things simply but well, paying attention to the minutest of details along the way. Of course, the men who built it had to be strong, shrewd and deeply versed in the mechanics of soccer. But all that would have counted for nothing without those more fundamental tenets which are as indispensable in life as in football.

Undoubtedly Bill Shankly had applied them, too, in his previous managerial posts at Carlisle, Grimsby, Workington and Huddersfield, where tangible success had been elusive. But those clubs, with all due respect, did not offer the same possibilities as Liverpool, where the place, the people, the club and the man himself effected a special chemistry.

In the decades ahead, the values set down and the philosophy propounded in 1959 would come to be epitomised by the Boot Room, a small and seemingly unremarkable chamber along the corridor from the dressing rooms at Anfield. At first, as the name implies, it was mainly a repository for boots and other kit which was used daily for training. But gradually, out of convenience, it became the place where the coaching staff would sit and thrash out the problems of the day, mull over the merits of training routines, tactics and performances, or simply exchange gossip. Shankly was not a regular denizen of the Boot Room; rather it was the domain of Paisley and Fagan, then later Moran and Roy Evans, Chris Lawler, Phil Thompson and others.

It became the place where visiting managers and coaches were entertained to a post-match drink, and around it grew a certain mystique. That unadorned, somewhat scruffy room entered soccer folklore as the nerve-centre of the Liverpool operation, an almost hallowed inner sanctum into which outsiders were hardly ever admitted, the dwelling place of soccer's equivalent of the holy grail.

In a way, it was appropriate. It was so workaday, so lacking in pretension, so honest - just like, in the good years, Liverpool FC itself. It was important not for what it was but for what it stood, and though it was no more than breeze blocks and mortar, when it was demolished during the traumatic and ill-starred reign of Graeme Souness, it was as though the living heart had been ripped out of the club.

The Boot Room is the title of this book, then, because it remains in the consciousness as a symbol of all that was best about Liverpool, and perhaps, it was reasonable to hope in the summer of 1994, what could be once more as the admirable combination of Roy Evans, Ronnie Moran and Doug Livermore began building for the future.

*Opposite: A king in his castle: Bob Paisley in the Boot Room with the League Championship trophy which spent so much time in his custody. His feet remained firmly connected to the ground, though. As he once remarked with memorable understatement: 'How could I get carried away? I've been here during the bad times - one year we finished second!'*

**'There I was, the Kirkby kid whose legs Bill Shankly**
**compared to a sparrow's. There he was, the messiah, an idol.**
**Yet every time I saw him he would say "How are ye eating?"**
**I would just stand there listening, making sure my shoulders were straight.**
**Then I would go home and tell my mum - He spoke to me today!'**

*Phil Thompson on Bill Shankly*

*Paris, 1981, and the Kirkby kid had come a long way. Liverpool skipper Phil Thompson with the European Cup.*

Bill Shankly is revered, and rightly so, as the man who built Liverpool FC. But the passage of time tends to obscure the truth that his achievement was neither instant nor a stately procession from one triumph to another. In fact, in those early years he had to battle every step of the way, and the main enemy was within Anfield. Before Shanks could take on the might of Everton, Tottenham Hotspur, Manchester United and the rest, he had to confront the creeping complacency which had condemned the Reds to a second-class existence throughout the latter half of the 1950s.

As well as the urgently-required physical refurbishment of Melwood and Anfield, Bill knew that a wholesale clear-out of players was demanded if Liverpool were to join the big league. Within a few weeks of his arrival he had drawn up a list of 24 footballers whose services he did not wish to retain, and within 12 months they had all gone. It should be emphasised, at this point, that while the majority departed because they did not pass muster, there were honourable exceptions. Most notable among these was the incomparable Billy Liddell, who retired at decade's end after a majestic career which stretched back to the war and whose name will be forever revered on Merseyside. But whatever the various reasons for individual exits, finding suitable replacements for so many men constituted a formidable task.

Of course, the principle of betterment was unarguable, it was the means which caused the problems. It was an inescapable fact that top footballers cost top money and, at first, the Liverpool board was not prepared to part with it. Attempts to prise Jack Charlton from Leeds United and Dave Mackay from Hearts (later he was snapped up for Tottenham by Bill Nicholson) foundered on parsimony, and there were moments when Bill Shankly despaired.

It seemed that Second Division safety and gates of around 30,000 were enough to keep the directors happy. Their attitude was one which might have been expected of a smaller club, but their manager knew it was just not good enough for Liverpool. Roger Hunt, who joined the club three months before Shankly's appointment, puts it like this: 'So many people seemed to be content just jogging along, doing reasonably well and never spending much on the transfer market. But Bill Shankly was different. He sensed what could be achieved and, as a passionate man himself, he felt keenly the passion and the longing of the fans.'

It's hard to believe in the light of what followed, but there were even moments when he contemplated leaving on principle. Long and heartfelt discussions with an old friend and fellow Scot, Matt Busby of Manchester United, went a long way towards convincing him that he should stay; so, of course, did his own natural aversion to quitting any job which he had started.

But it was the arrival on the board of Eric Sawyer, one of the leading financial brains of the mega-successful Littlewoods Pools company, which proved a decisive factor. He shared Shankly's belief in the limitless potential of their club and, most importantly, was ready to spend money in the process of realising it.

Thus, after the Reds had finished third in the Second Division in both 1959/60 and 1960/61, the manager spoke of his burning desire to sign Motherwell centre-forward Ian St John, who was available for £37,500. Certain directors counselled caution, saying they could not afford to buy him; Eric Sawyer proved his mettle, averring that Liverpool couldn't afford NOT to sign the man who would be dubbed 'The Saint'. A few months later, he displayed similar vision in backing Shankly's quest for a massive young centre-half, Ron Yeats of Dundee United, who

*Opposite:*
*The messiah among his own: Bill Shankly joins the fans to celebrate the 1973 title triumph. Over his right shoulder can be glimpsed a young and joyful Phil Thompson. They were two men from different generations but who shared the same Red view of the world.*

cost £30,000. Now the cornerstones of Bill's first great side, indeed of the Liverpool empire that was to reign for a quarter of a century, were in place.

All the while, and even more importantly, the manager had been imbuing his sense of values throughout the club and finding out what made people tick. Early on he decreed that the road runs which had formed a major plank of the previous regime's training methods should cease. He pointed out that the game was played with a ball on grass; therefore, he added with devastating simplicity, the players should spend the bulk of their preparation time on grass with a ball at their feet.

To that end, five-a-side games became of paramount importance and grew into a Liverpool institution. He reasoned that they re-created every situation that would crop up in a match, as well as putting the players through the same physical demands that would face them on a Saturday. Shanks, Reuben Bennett, Bob Paisley and Joe Fagan used to take part, usually in games between the staff and the youngsters.

As Ronnie Moran recalls, the boss used to love every minute of them: 'He really threw himself into those games; they meant so much to him. He was the centre of the action - and if he was injured or ill (which was extremely rare) we wouldn't play, it was as simple as that. I don't think he could bear to watch the rest playing football if he couldn't join in. He was in his fifties but still a very useful performer. He had never lost his body-swerve, often dipping his shoulder and just going past a young opponent. He would do things on the ball I would never even attempt!'

Phil Thompson, too, remembers the Melwood five-a-sides with almost reverential affection. By the time he had arrived as a gawky but spirited hopeful, it was the late 1960s and the end of Shanks' first marvellous era, but in essence nothing had changed.

The man who went on to captain club and country, then later return to Anfield to coach the reserves, glowed with pleasure as he reminisced: 'Those games took place at the end of every day's training, perhaps for the last half-hour or so. They were always called five-a-sides even if there were six, seven or eight on each team. Shanks would lead the staff against the kids and, just before we played, he would be looking over at us, rubbing his hands with relish of what was in store, almost as if he were on edge at the kick-off of some big match.

For the moment that game was the most important thing on earth to him. People think it's a tall tale, but it was really true that he never finished on the losing side, that if his team were losing then the game continued until they got in front. Playing for the staff, usually, were Bill, Bob, Joe, Ronnie, Reuben and maybe Tom Saunders (who arrived as youth development officer at the end of the decade). On most occasions the staff would win comfortably enough in 30, maybe 45 minutes, but if they didn't then it went on as long as was necessary.

Nobody took penalties for his side except Shanks. He absolutely loved it. He placed the ball very deliberately, then walked back with a swagger and crashed it in. He never failed - if the goalie saved it then he had moved too soon and it would be retaken!'

Phil believed the idea of the games was to test the kids, to see how they would react to different situations. 'That way they found out a lot about each lad. Did he hide? Was he lazy? Five-a-sides were also a brilliant test of ability; they were very quick and your touch and passing had to be good.'

'It was important to get really involved to enhance your career. Occasionally I would play on the staff team, which was a great honour. I was a runner, I never knew when to stop - pushing and shoving and harrying. Later they told me they saw a bit in me because of that, though I could play a bit as well!'

Phil marvelled at Shankly's ability to find time for everyone, even though he was so busy and everything at the club centred on him: 'He was wonderful with the boys, a real father figure. In fact, he seemed to take more personal interest in them than in the first team. There I was, the Kirkby kid whose legs he compared to a sparrow's. There he was, the messiah, an idol. Yet every time he saw me he would say: "How are ye, son? Did ye sleep well? How are

*The sort of moment that made all the Boot Room planning worthwhile. Roger Hunt (left) has scored a last-minute equaliser in the Merseyside derby at Goodison Park in September 1962. Kevin Lewis (centre), who laid on the goal, advances for a celebratory embrace.*

ye eating?" I would stand there listening, making sure my shoulders were straight. Then I would go home and tell my mum - HE spoke to me today.'

Attention to detail, the personal touch, genuine concern for the young men in his care, an all-consuming passion for the job - they were all facets of the Shankly doctrine and all played their part in the Reds' continuing glory. However, there have been decent and enthusiastic men at every club, but only Liverpool have achieved so much. Clearly, there must have been more to the 'secret' of their success. It is time to examine the rules Bill Shankly laid down for playing the game.

*Billy Liddell, whose illustrious career was drawing to a close as Shankly arrived. Billy was as fine a footballer as any man to pull on the red shirt, before or since. What a shame that his prime did not coincide with a successful Liverpool side*

*Maestro and loyal disciple, united in tension. Bill Shankly on the bench with Ronnie Moran, waiting for the final whistle in the second leg of the 1973 UEFA Cup Final against Borussia Moenchengladbach. The Reds won 3-2 on aggregate to record Bill's first European triumph. Ronnie says of his former leader: 'I learned more in my first three months under him than in the rest of my career.'*

**'No one was asked to do more than anyone else... we were a team.
We shared the ball, we shared the game, we shared the worries.'**

*Bill Shankly on the Liverpool way*

Bill Shankly possessed strong socialist ideals which dictated the way he lived his life and were reflected in the way his team played football. He employed a collective system in which there was no room for temperamental prima donnas and in which each man worked for his mates while receiving similar support in return. Written down, it seems devastatingly simple and Bill maintained that was how it should be. He could never understand the urge by many modern coaches to complicate the game. 'It's madness. It won't get them anywhere,' he used to say, and the success of Liverpool was an all-powerful argument to reinforce his view.

Ronnie Moran recalls one coaching get-together which the great man was required to attend. He was lectured on some new training method called 'shadow play', which involved players chasing each other about the pitch without the ball. Anything that didn't involve the ball was anathema to Shankly, who had one tucked under his arm as he listened sceptically to the speaker's theories. 'Then he looked up at the sky, turned to this coach and said: "Hey, we can't have shadow-play, there's no sun. Let's have a five-a-side instead!"'

The Liverpool method, built up over the years, involved groups of players ferrying the ball out from the back in a succession of short, early, accurate passes. To make it work fluidly involved constant running off the ball to provide passing options for the man in possession and, of course, it demanded total mastery of the game's basic skills.

Bill didn't expect all his players to be capable of dribbling past a line of defenders, but he did expect them all to be able to control the ball instantly and pass it accurately. In addition, the capacity to improvise, to make the most of any fleeting opportunities created along the way, was compulsory.

It was a way of playing in which the manager had always held faith and its efficacy was underlined by the Reds' encounters with top European sides. Despite his much-reported mistrust of all things foreign - at least some of which was tongue-in-cheek - he studied the Continentals intently and learned much from their approach to the game.

He would say: 'You can't score until you've got the ball, so when you've got it you must keep it. That might mean playing cat and mouse for a long time, switching the ball around and apparently not getting very far; but then, suddenly, an opening will appear.' He believed the constant pit-pat interchanges could lull opponents into a false sense of security, confuse them into dropping their guard, thus setting them up for the killer thrust. It was deceptively, often destructively simple and, because the players were operating what amounted to a relay system of passing, it was delightfully economical in terms of energy conservation.

Despite being criticised unfairly by some pundits as predictable automatons during the 1960s, Liverpool had employed a precise passing game throughout the Shankly reign, though it became more pronounced in his latter years after several seasons of European competition. By the early 1970s Bill's central defenders, Phil Thompson and Emlyn Hughes, would hoof a long ball upfield only when under severe pressure or if a specific opening had been spotted.

This development signalled the end at the club for Larry Lloyd, a big stopper from the old-fashioned mould, though to his credit he rose to new heights - and regained his England place - with Nottingham Forest. In future, especially at Anfield, footballing centre-halves such as Alan Hansen and Mark Lawrenson would become the norm.

Yet despite boasting players of such ability, Liverpool never encouraged them to run with the ball out of defence into the other half. 'That's running in no-man's land and it's nonsense. There's no need for it. It just gives the other side the chance to take it away from you. Why

*Irrepressible glee radiated frequently from the features of Emlyn Hughes, thanks to triumphs such as the lifting of the 1976 UEFA Cup, pictured here. Hughes, the first new boy to earn a regular place in Shankly's wonderful side of the mid-1960s, was an accomplished all-rounder who resorted to hoofing the ball only under the direst pressure.*

*Opposite:
The man who shot down Real Madrid: Alan Kennedy with the European Cup after his goal won the 1981 final against the exalted Spaniards. Alan was required to revolutionise his playing style after moving from Newcastle to Liverpool, and the Anfield coaches earned his undying admiration.*

give them that?' Shanks grated.

Bill contended, also, that because no one was expected to sprint the length of the field to score a goal, then no one was subjecting themselves to overdue strain and injuries were less likely. Thus, at least in theory, the game became easier and safer for all concerned and the common cause was served by the side's consequent success.

Truly, it was socialism on the pitch. As Bill explained in later years: 'No one was asked to do more than anyone else . . . we were a team. We shared the ball, we shared the game, we shared the worries. No one had to do it on his own.'

A virtue almost as dear to Shankly's heart as solidarity was patience, the need for which he preached endlessly: '90 minutes is a long time. I told the players that our plans might take 80 minutes to come to fruition, they might take 89, but we must keep going. The number of goals we scored in the last five minutes of matches was unbelievable over the years. It was heartbreaking to the opposition, of course, but patience was always one of the most important aspects of our game.'

Bill was a great believer in team pattern, too, and of every member being intimately acquainted with that pattern. It would mystify him when he watched another side to discover that they had no comparable method, that the players didn't seem to know what they were doing, where they were running and why.

'I knew that if one of our players was in a situation where he needed help, then somebody would help him. We never complicated tasks. We gave players something easy to understand, then they got on with their specific jobs.' He compared it to members of a workforce being on speaking terms, rather than being forced to do their jobs as total strangers. Each man knew what his team-mate would do in any given circumstance and the

*Alan Hansen, arguably the finest example of the footballing centre-halves who became the Anfield norm. Here Alan looks moderately pleased after scoring against his fellow Scots, Aberdeen, during the successful European Cup campaign of 1981.*

team ran smoothly because of that knowledge. This was in stark contrast to many other clubs, where star players were a law unto themselves, and where the side foundered when key men were absent.

Shankly's ceaseless search for every tiny wrinkle which might give his team a priceless edge extended to ensuring that each man got a touch of the ball as early as possible in every match. He explained: 'It might be something very simple, just chesting it down and passing it to a team-mate. It doesn't look much but it's something. Even the briefest of touches, if it's a good one, helps to build confidence.'

He stressed to his charges repetitively - Shanks never shrunk from repetition when he knew he was talking sense - that it was better than trying something fancy early on which, if it didn't come off, would tend to drain self-belief.

Ostensibly, then, the Liverpool way of playing was simple to learn, but not everyone found it easy to assimilate and it required deceptively skilful coaching to impart.

A case in point was that of full-back Alan Kennedy who, after his £330,000 transfer from Newcastle United in August 1978, had to adjust to a vastly different style of play to that to which he had grown accustomed on Tyneside.

He amplifies: 'When I got the ball at Newcastle, the idea was to hit the farthest forward black-and-white shirt. Usually that was Malcolm Macdonald, steaming through the middle to run on to the ball, a tactic by which he scored so many of his goals. Then, after making the pass, there was a tendency to stand and watch what Malcolm made of it.

'At Liverpool it was completely different. I was told to give the ball to the nearest red shirt and then to move. Whatever else, I must never stand still. This was a huge change for me and I admit it took me some time to mend my ways. Ronnie Moran used to tell me till he was blue in the face, but old habits die hard and in the heat of the action I would sometimes hit a long ball. Of course, that was extremely frustrating for our midfielders, who had run into position to receive from me.

'Gradually I got the message. If Ray Kennedy or Steve Heighway were wide, I just had to push the ball to them and then support them. When we were attacking, I wasn't expected to cut inside. My job was to slip outside to provide that extra option, then get my cross in, and then get back.

'I have to say, though, that imparting what was essentially a simple message was not always a simple task. Particularly in retrospect, the coaches have my undying admiration.'

Alan explains that much of the instruction took the form of personal advice, rather than the practising of intricate movements: 'We had good players and they had command of the basic skills. We did lots of keep-ball in training, which offered realistic match situations and that stood us in good stead.'

Ian Callaghan, who epitomised all that was best about Liverpool in a senior career which stretched from 1960 to 1978, still marvels at the sheer constancy and timelessness of Bill Shankly's methods and values.

'Our collective style never varied. Whatever new players came along, people like Kevin Keegan and Steve Heighway, they were always able to slot into the tried and tested system. Bill, Bob Paisley and Joe Fagan saw to it that each man maximised his strengths and used those strengths to the utmost benefit of the team. With such a steady approach, and so much accumulated wisdom, it was difficult to see how it would ever end. But nothing lasts forever.'

**'Some people might think we were lazy, but that was fine. Let them!
What's the point of tearing players to pieces in the first few days?'**

*Bill Shankly on pre-season training*

Throughout the Anfield reign of Bill Shankly, he maintained that his Liverpool were the fittest team in the First Division. They had to be to chase and harry the way they did from first whistle to last, scoring so many of their goals in the dying embers of games, when the minds of tiring opponents were turning, perhaps, towards the sanctuary of a hot bath and the enjoyment of a cool beer.

'It's incredible what you can achieve if you're fit - and if you're young and strong there's never any excuse for not being fit,' he would rasp, with a glint in his eye that left no vestige of a doubt that slackers would not be given the time of day, much less a place in the side.

The very thought of pre-season training under such a demanding taskmaster was daunting, indeed, with visions of sand dunes and assault courses easy to conjure up. Certainly July was a murderous month for footballers at most clubs, so what must it be like at run-all-day Liverpool?

In fact, therein lay a fascinating paradox and one of the most superficially surprising, yet - on closer examination - logical explanations for the Reds' continued pre-eminence. When they reported back for duty after the summer break, the players were not training for a campaign that began the next week or even that month. They were working towards achieving peak condition for their first League match and that would be some five weeks hence.

Accordingly, they began steadily, cautiously, anxious to avoid undue strain on bodies that had been resting on beaches or in back gardens. Those first sessions would involve nothing more than an easy jog, perhaps a gentle five-a-side. Make no mistake, the hard work would come, but it would come later, when they were ready. Until then not a sprint would be made, not a weight would be lifted, not even a ball kicked in anger.

England centre-forward David Johnson was mightily impressed by the Liverpool training methods after he arrived from Ipswich Town for £200,000 in 1976. He says: 'At many other clubs they try to get you fit on the first day after the holiday. It would almost kill you - running up and down hills, going through every ferocious exercise imaginable to man. It was sheer torture from a standing start, and most bodies couldn't take it. So over four or five weeks you would miss half the programme because you had suffered some strain-induced injury or were too stiff to move. If you did get through it, then you were absolutely knackered by the end of it.

'But at Liverpool they had just one thing in mind: bringing you to a natural peak for the first game. To that end they built up the activity gradually, enabling all the players, providing they did not meet with some unlucky mishap, to get through every minute of pre-season training. I managed that in each of my six pre-seasons at the club.'

It was a commonsense approach instituted by Shankly, then carried on through subsequent successful regimes but which, staggeringly, continued not to be the rule elsewhere. Indeed, some outsiders sneered at the 'soft' build-up, but Shanks didn't care in the least: 'Some people might think we were lazy, but that's fine. Let them! What's the point of tearing players to pieces in the first few days? We never bothered with sand dunes and hills and roads; we trained on grass, where football is played.'

As he called for patience during matches, so he preached it in the battle for peak fitness. He pointed out that over-laborious work in July and August could induce stress-related maladies which don't become apparent until later in the season, often at crucial junctures. One year, he reckoned, such an injury caused Ray Clemence to miss two games which, arguably, cost Liverpool the Championship. The manager believed it had been brought on by excessive efforts to improve the goalkeeper's rather moderate dead-ball kicking. In future, that exercise was cut from his pre-season routine; Ray worked at his weakness, all right, but not until his all-round fitness was at a level to cope with the strenuous effort.

Johnson believes such attention to detail in the Reds' preparation was massively instrumental in achieving such long-lasting sway over their rivals. He cites another persuasive example. Despite having developed splendid facilities at their Melwood training ground, Liverpool continued to use Anfield as a weekday base. Until Graeme Souness decreed otherwise in the early 1990s, the players would report there each morning, then take a coach to Melwood before returning to the stadium for a shower and, if they wanted it, a light meal.

Why, asked David rhetorically, did the club persist with the practice so long instead of adopting the seemingly less complicated procedure of having the players make their own way to and from the training ground, thus obviating the need to go to Anfield?

It made sense, he reckons, for three excellent reasons: 'First, everybody got used to Anfield as a working environment. That meant it was not unfamiliar on a Saturday when you arrived for the match. It was your workplace, you were there every day, you'd have your own peg in the dressing-room. You knew all the non-footballing staff and there was a bit of banter; a family atmosphere grew up.'

'It was just a little thing, but it took away a degree of stress that any change in surroundings is likely to produce. Hence you would be more relaxed and better able to perform well on the pitch. When I was at Everton we went to Goodison only on matchdays, an experience twice as nerve-wracking as it might have been.'

David's second point related to improved fitness. 'If you strip and shower immediately after training, as you tend to do if you have driven to the training ground, it is a pretty swift process but one which is not really suited to athletes, who need a lengthy cooling-down period. Your body temperature takes about 40 minutes to drop after heavy exercise, so you would still be sweating after your shower; your pores would remain open and you would be more susceptible to chills and strains.'

The old way, he reckoned, was much better: winding down with a cup of tea and a chat, then a 20-minute coach ride back to Anfield, and only *then*, some three-quarters of an hour after training had stopped, would the players take their showers.

Bill Shankly swore by this routine: 'If you have a bath or a shower ten minutes after hard work then you'll carry on sweating all day. There's nothing worse than sitting around sweating, it's bad for your system. It doesn't seem much but it was very important to us . . .

*Good humour reigns in the Anfield directors box prior to a late 1960s visit by Manchester United. Bill Shankly, of course, holds centre stage while United's Jimmy Murphy (bottom left) reaches back to shake hands with Joe Fagan. Bob Paisley grins away to Shanks' right while the front row is completed by a youthful Martin Edwards (United's current chairman), and his father Louis, who filled the role at the time. Pipe-smoking on the left is Cliff Lloyd of the PFA.*

nothing Liverpool did was silly.'

If proof of the theory were needed, it was provided in 1970 when rebuilding work on the main stand made it more convenient for the players to report direct to Melwood each morning. In the months that followed, the Reds suffered one of the worst spates of injuries the club had ever known. Some might have called it coincidence, but not in Bill's hearing . . .

The third advantage David Johnson mentions is that the daily coach journeys were good for morale, the inevitable high jinks and leg-pulling fostering togetherness. 'All little things, nothing earth-shattering, but add them all up and they were worth a lot,' he concludes.

That strong team spirit was very much in evidence at Melwood throughout the reigns of Shankly, Paisley and Fagan. There can be no doubt that hard graft was the order of the day, but it took place in a positive and flexible atmosphere.

Johnson says that during his spell at the club, in the Paisley era, training was almost invariably enjoyable. The Liverpool coaches never employed the worthy but dull routines favoured by many clubs, where exercises devised to highlight players' deficiencies tended to leave precious little time for anything else. David shuddered as he conjured up a vision of how not to retain players' interest: 'It can end up like going to school and attending the class you hate most - and that's every day!'

In contrast, the Melwood sessions were distinguished by the coaching staff's imagination. The five-a-sides beloved of Shankly remained the principal training vehicle, but even they could become stereotyped without plenty of variety. To achieve this, Messrs Fagan and Moran would change the teams frequently, ever ready to adapt to the mood of the players and the needs of the side for the next match.

Moran elucidates: 'You always have your plans when you start, but sometimes, within a few minutes, you pick up that it's not right for that day. Instead of persevering with something that's wrong, we think on our feet. That's just common sense.'

Ronnie, who has worked with the first team since 1974, has trained alongside his charges down the years, playing in the same games and doing the same exercises, finding he can communicate with them better that way than by screaming from the touchline. He never attempts to alter the natural style of an individual, merely seeks to imbue good habits and direct every ounce of talent in the right direction.

He continues: 'If he wasn't a good footballer in the first place then he wouldn't be here. If we suddenly decide someone we have bought or developed is not up to it then we are, in effect, criticising our own judgement.'

Phil Thompson, himself a member of the coaching line-up between 1986 and 1992 - running a vibrant reserve team and nurturing the likes of Robbie Fowler and Steve McManaman in the process - confirms that these enlightened methods brought the best out of people.

'We didn't spend a lot of time working slavishly at things, certainly not set pieces. We didn't have to. Our players were all well educated in a football sense, so they knew how to react to various situations and play whatever was on, which almost always involved transferring the ball to the nearest red shirt.

We were treated like adults and expected to use our heads to exploit the opposition's weaknesses. Any new players found this out at once; they had to slot into our way without fuss. We didn't want prima donnas who had to go their own way. Kenny Dalglish, for example, was just right for Liverpool. He had wonderful ability, being able to take balls in to his feet and either lay them off straight away or retain possession and turn. Absolutely perfect.'

Alan Kennedy, like most ex-Reds, had huge respect for the club's senior coaching team, all of whom could dispense discipline when it was required but who had the good sense to look the other way at times, particularly when things were going well (almost always!).

'Usually the first-teamers were supervised by some combination of Bob, Joe and Ronnie,'

*Opposite:*
*Satisfied with a job well done: Kenny Dalglish relaxes in the Anfield dressing room after Liverpool had clinched the League Championship of 1980. With his ability to take balls to feet, Kenny was perfect for Liverpool's sweet-passing style.*

he recalls, 'but sometimes they would leave us to get on with it while they went off for a five-a-side with the youngsters. Then we might lark around a bit, playing walking-football or piggy-back football. They'd look across and see us but often wouldn't intervene. We'd have done our hardest work by then, anyway, and the spirit was great, so they allowed us a bit of latitude. It's called man-management and it worked.

Mind you, it was very different if we had just lost a game. Then Joe and Ronnie could be extremely harsh. Ironically, they used to take it out on the reserves, making them lap the training ground. In fact, if you didn't know our last result, that was how you could tell - if we'd been beaten, the young lads would be running their socks off! We'd have to sweat a bit, too, then at the end of the session the first team would have a chat about what had gone wrong.'

In his day, too, Shanks had been keen on minute post-match analysis in the wake of a defeat, gathering the players in the big lounge at Anfield on a Monday afternoon. Everyone was encouraged to have their say and punches were not pulled. Such discussions, he believed, were healthy and productive: 'We found we could learn more from losing than from winning,' he maintained.

Thus the basic tenets of Bill's soccer gospel remained in place at Liverpool, right through the periods of his two immediate successors, Bob Paisley and Joe Fagan, and, with minor adaptations as the game began to change along with the times, into the Kenny Daglish era.

Even today, some of Bill's 'torture boards' are still in place at Melwood, though they are not used as frequently or as intensely as they were in the 1960s. He used the movable wooden boards to keep the ball in play during a series of exercises which honed players' dribbling, shooting and trapping techniques at the same time as developing their strength and stamina.

The routines took a lot of getting used to and new players tended to find them shattering, building themselves up gradually until they could keep pace with their team-mates. Utility man Geoff Strong, a £40,000 'steal' from Arsenal in November 1964, and big centre-forward Tony Hateley, who cost £96,000 from Chelsea in the summer of 1967, were two men who found Shankly's system of 'exhaustion and recovery' - what a world of expression he put into those two words - particularly, well, exhausting. But they both came to terms with it and were more effective members of the team in consequence. As Bill put it, after surviving the boards, playing football was the easiest thing in the world!

But despite Shanks' utter dedication to the fitness ethic, he applied it with restraint and meticulous judgement. Indeed, he was acutely aware of the dangers of overdoing physical preparation, not only at the start of a season (as already mentioned) but at any time. He would stress that it was not how long a player trained that mattered, but how well he trained. As little as 35 minutes per day, properly used, could be enough for some individuals, though it was impossible to generalise.

Workaholics such as Ian Callaghan or Kevin Keegan had to be told, on occasion, to take it easy. They never knew how to give less than 100 per-cent effort at all times, so there was a fear that they might burn themselves out. Others, who had better remain nameless, required a periodic metaphorical kick up the bum to keep them on the road to fitness.

Shanks saw over-training as a particular danger to young players, which he reckoned was a major factor in so many schoolboy internationals failing to make the professional grade. Furthermore he abhorred a vogue adopted by some clubs for two stints a day. It was something of a hobby horse to the Liverpool boss, who declared: 'I don't believe in it. If you do that then both sessions have to be easy, and what's the point in that? It's not doing any good if the players get tired or bored. You end up making them sick of the game.'

Over-coaching, also, came in for heavy criticism from Anfield's soccer sage, who thought much of the modern teaching was too reliant on jargon. 'The boys have got to know what you're talking about, or they'll get mixed up.' It all came down to his central, unyielding belief that football was a simple game and that to complicate it was a crime. When Bill Shankly was holding forth on that theme, it took a brave man to argue with him!

*Opposite:*
*Ray Clemence, the brilliant goalkeeper whose goal-kicking constituted a slight weakness and whose efforts to overcome it might have caused an injury. To some, it might have seemed a comparatively minor detail; to Shankly and company, it was a matter requiring instant attention.*

**'It was absolutely sacrosanct.  All the press lads knew
that was one threshold they didn't cross without an invite
- and that had to come from the top men'**

*Photographer Steve Hale's view of the Boot Room*

I t was nothing elaborate. It was tiny, scruffy and suffused with a distinctive musty smell in which sweat was a major component. Yet to a whole generation of football folk, the Anfield Boot Room was the holiest of holy inner sanctums, the place where wise and venerated men plotted the continued dominance of the English game. In short, it was the very hub of Liverpool FC.

To pass through the portals of that humble 12ft by 12ft compartment was classed as an honour and it was conferred on very few outsiders. Even celebrities from the world of entertainment, more accustomed to luxury and well used to privilege, reacted with awe when invited in for a drink and a natter.

As Phil Thompson says: 'It was so ordinary, yet it gave off so much charisma and character. The Americans would have paid thousands to take it apart and ship it home brick by brick. Invariably, people who went in for the first time were thrilled. The looks on their faces would say it all - it was as though they had been blessed from on high. They couldn't have been more pleased if they'd been asked inside Buckingham Palace.'

The Boot Room - somehow it seems appropriate to use capital letters - became the symbol of the Reds' homely, down-to-earth appeal, far removed from the glamorous images of, say, Manchester United, Arsenal or even Everton.

In truth, the media built it up out of all proportion, investing in it a heady combination of mystique and exclusivity, creating for it a timeless identity as the place where reposed soccer's most sacred secret, that of apparently never-ending success.

All this could hardly have been imagined when, back in the early days of Bill Shankly's management, Bob Paisley, Reuben Bennett and Joe Fagan adopted it as a cosy and convenient spot to chew the fat after training. Situated next to the kit-drying room, it was warm, often uncomfortably so, but it served a useful purpose.

Ronnie Moran's first memories of the little chamber are of Shanks' three lieutenants going inside and closing the door: 'I was still playing at the time, but there was never any big deal about the Boot Room. It was just used for the kit in those days and had no other significance. Later on, of course, visiting managers and coaches would be asked in for a drink after the game, and that was when it became well-known.'

Phil Thompson carries fascinatingly contrasting memories of the Boot Room, both as a kind of 'headmaster's study' in his time as a player and then, when he coached the reserves, as a place in which a large segment of his everyday working life was spent.

The likeable Liverpudlian, whose first-team Anfield career stretched from 1971 to 1982 and included a momentous spell as skipper, recalls that players didn't venture inside without an invitation. 'It was definitely out of bounds most of the time, and if you were asked in then you knew there must be a problem to sort out. The invitation would come from Joe or Ronnie. They wouldn't make a big thing of it, but you would know it was serious.'

Such a summons might involve a preliminary discussion before the matter went to the manager, but more often than not a quiet chat in the Boot Room was enough to resolve it without involving the boss. It was a sensible, down-to-earth system - and it worked.

Sammy Lee, the Liverpool and England midfielder who joined the club's coaching staff during Graeme Souness' time as manager, confirms that liberties could never be taken anywhere in the vicinity of the hallowed portals: 'The only time most of us would go near the Boot Room was to knock on the door and collect a pair of boots. Normally we would give it a pretty wide berth. Even if you just walked past you knew there was a fair chance that Ronnie

*Opposite: Kenny Dalglish, flanked here by Ronnie Moran (left) and Roy Evans, spent less time in the Boot Room than his immediate predecessors as Liverpool manager, but always he treated the revered bolt-hole with the utmost respect.*

*The last walk: Bill Shankly leads out Liverpool to meet Leeds United in the 1974 Charity Shield at Wembley, the final big game before his retirement. To his right is Brian Clough, who survived just 44 days at Elland Road but who more than made up for that elsewhere. Clough was not a regular partaker in Boot Room hospitality, but always sent an apology for his absences.*

*Back in 1974 it was rare for the unassuming Joe Fagan to step into the spotlight. This was an exception as Joe (centre) lifts the FA Cup on Liverpool's triumphant tour of the city. Also on board (left to right) are Emlyn Hughes, Bob Paisley, Kevin Keegan and Ray Clemence.*

would catch sight of you and call you a bastard - even if we'd beaten one of the best teams in the country in our last match. It was always the same, one of the many ways in which the management made sure we kept our feet on the ground.'

Ian Callaghan, holder of the club's appearance record, underlines the regard in which the Boot Room and its regular occupants were held: 'I didn't go inside often during the early part of my career but later on, being friendly with Roy Evans, I would pop in for the occasional beer. I never just walked in, though. That would have been out of order.

All the players had so much respect for the coaching staff and what they stood for. They were such ordinary people, completely honest and so effective at what they did. The most important thing was that, no matter how you played, if you gave 100 per cent every week they would have respect for you.'

The coaches would repair directly to their 'retreat' straight after training, invariably embarking on an informal but exhaustive examination of all football-related topics of the day, principally those raised by the just-completed session at Melwood.

Phil Thompson again: 'They would talk about the day's five-a-sides, perhaps whether a certain player was pulling his weight, maybe whether another was as fit as they'd like him to be. They might agree that one man needed a bit of extra pressure while they should lay off another. They looked at the whole squad like a collection of agony aunts. There was a lot of psychology involved.'

It was there, too, that the famous Anfield notebooks were compiled, priceless volumes in which were contained scrupulously detailed records on each player. That was yet another tradition begun by Shankly years before. Bill wrote in his autobiography: 'I have many notebooks, accumulated over the years, which are filled with information. I picked up something from everybody in football I came into contact with, no matter who they were. If they did something or said something I thought was good it would go down in the book. Whether or not they were conscious of what I was doing, I don't know. At home and abroad I would look and listen and think: "That's not bad but I'll add that to it and I'll cut this out of it."'

Such a goldmine of information proved invaluable in countless situations thereafter. Whenever something went wrong, whether major or minor, the manager could come up with a similar situation from his notebooks and proceed accordingly.

The notebooks compiled by the men who followed him were, perhaps, less wide-ranging, confining themselves mainly to each day's training session, which was documented in minute detail. As a result the staff could look up the performance and state of fitness of any Liverpool player on any day for years past. The books would even reveal each man's dietary requirements, the particular training routines employed and their effect, even whether it rained or the sun was shining.

Thus, like their mentor before them, Messrs Paisley, Fagan, Moran and company were never short of a precedent. The mere phrase 'attention to detail' does not begin to convey the utterly comprehensive nature of the method. Of course, the records are confidential and will ever remain so, but what riveting reading they would make if published - a unique, warts-and-all chronicle of the most successful era any English club has ever enjoyed.

Those bulging, penned notebooks were not, as might be imagined, locked away in some top-security vault, but stacked unceremoniously in a Boot Room cupboard. Possibly their very presence contributed to the 'untouchable' aura surrounding the room, which was observed by every player on *almost* every occasion. Just once in a while, when there was no one about, a practical joker would slip inside, but with nothing more devious in mind than embellishing one of the dog-eared team groups that adorned the wall. In this way, the likeness of Ronnie Moran might acquire devil's horns, spectacles, or even a full head of hair!

Non-footballing folk who craved entry would wait outside in the corridor, more in hope than expectation. Phil recalls that in his playing days he would occasionally take visitors on a tour of Anfield - 'Thompson's Tours' as his team-mates called them - but it was extremely rare that the Boot Room was included.

Photographer Steve Hale, whose work has taken him to Anfield throughout the past quarter of a century, gives an illuminating outsider's view: 'The Boot Room was absolutely sacrosanct. All the press lads knew that was one threshold they didn't cross without an invite - and that had to come from one of the top men, one of those whose say really mattered.

I got in a few times, usually to take a picture of players with a trophy. Another time was when Ian Rush returned to Liverpool from Juventus and I took a picture of him with John Barnes. Even when you were inside, it was not a place to take liberties. You knew, without the point being laboured, that you were not free to start snapping all over the place. You felt you were privileged to be there at all and to abuse that privilege would have been absolutely out of the question. That was where the business of running Liverpool was done - and whatever went on in there remained strictly Liverpool's business.'

The chosen few who did gain admission were greeted by a scene which was anything but imposing. It was scruffy and untidy, evidence that even the cleaners were granted limited admittance. The boots of first-team and reserve players were hung on pegs along the wall, while underneath were collected boots which were awaiting either repair or the dustbin. There were also a couple of hamper-style kit skips, which were used as seats, and some metal garage-style shelving containing spare training kit.

As well as old soccer photographs, the walls were adorned by calendars which were exceedingly popular with a variety of visiting managers and, most certainly, the photographs they contained had little to do with football!

Also on display for many years was a progress wallchart for season 1978/79, on which Ronnie Moran, never one to dispense praise too lightly, had written a number of curmudgeonly comments about various performances. That term the Reds topped the table by eight points, quite an achievement in the days of two points for a win, yet still Ronnie demanded improvement.

However, despite this outward display of irascibility, there was a note against one springtime fixture which offered a hint at the deep satisfaction he must, in truth, have been feeling. It read, quite simply: 'Just like Real Madrid.' Enough said.

Just along from the wallchart were two cupboards, one containing the notebooks and a selection of Rothmans Football Yearbooks, the other doing duty as the drinks cabinet. In keeping with the surroundings, it was anything but posh, but it was an integral part of the legend which grew up around Boot Room hospitality.

It's not easy to comprehend now, but in the 1950s and 1960s there was little social contact between people at different clubs. It was another world, particularly for players, in the era before Ronnie Moran hung up his boots.

He remembers: 'You would play the game, shake hands with your opponents and not see them until you played the return match later in the season. Now players have their own lounge where they meet for drinks after showering and changing. The new way is much better for the game. It keeps players together and can go a long way towards calming people down after a flare-up on the field.'

That applies to coaches, too, of course, and the Boot Room offered a calm haven for them to cool down after letting off steam. Phil Thompson looks back with affection at some of Moran's own verbal excesses.

'Sometimes he tended to go over the top a bit during the game, having a real go at the opposition. But no matter how much the opposing coaches argued and slagged each other off in the dugout, the hospitality was always the same after the match - and that was whether we had won, drawn or lost. Liverpool men were always honourable in defeat. It was the same later on, when I was coaching. If we lost we would be strong and brave, and Ronnie set a great example.'

Phil grins appreciatively as he conjures up a post-match image of Moran, one far removed from the intimidating growler who had spent the afternoon or evening leaping up and down on the bench. In the aftermath, if anyone from the other side ventured a sheepish apology for their own heated words, he would smile broadly and say 'Hey, it doesn't matter, that's football. Now let's have a drink.' The earlier vehemence, which could be alarming to people who didn't know him, was no more than an expression of his passion for the game.

Roy Evans, who became Liverpool manager in 1994, spent many years alongside Ronnie on the bench, and he bears witness to the manner in which temperatures could rise in the dugout, a fact to which the vast majority of fans remain oblivious. 'Oh, there can be some very big arguments which would sound really bitter to outsiders. People can be screaming at each other, ready to tear each other's faces off. But once the game is over, that's history. It's all part of professional football.'

On the subject of the Boot Room drinks - a tradition which began at Anfield in the early 1970s and which has been copied since by most clubs - there is a widely-told story that Brian Clough snubbed the socialising. Roy, though, is quick to refute it. 'He came in and joined us during his time with Derby, rather more occasionally when he was at Forest, and when he didn't he always sent his apologies. There was no question of him ignoring us, as some people have suggested.'

In fact, it's possible that Clough availed himself rarely of the conviviality because he didn't want his brains picked. Legend has it that the hosts would dispense the refreshments, then casually turn the conversation around to what promising youngsters might be abroad in the lower divisions. If a visitor dropped a name then he was unwise, indeed, for it's a fair bet that the footballer concerned would be investigated in the near future by Liverpool's chief scout!

The principal refreshment on offer was Scotch or cans of lager. There might be gin if a visiting manager had expressed a preference, but brandy was rarely an option, probably only if a bottle had been donated.

Now and then, at times of celebration, the room could become uncomfortably crowded. Ronnie remembers one evening when some 40 people were crammed inside, shoulder to shoulder, with barely room to lift their glasses. That, though, was a rare exception, the essential exclusivity being rarely breached.

Gradually, fed by the Reds' continuing success, the legend of the Boot Room grew. For those who knew it best, no matter how high they climbed in the Anfield hierarchy, it remained a blessed bolt-hole. Both Bob Paisley and Joe Fagan, two of its 'founder fathers', used it regularly after they each became manager in their turn, preferring its easy familiarity to the plusher surroundings of the boss's office. Later Kenny Dalglish, a different breed who preferred dispensing hospitality within his own enclave upstairs, nevertheless treated the Boot Room with respect and it continued to flourish in his reign.

The end came under Graeme Souness, who presided over its demolition as part of a massive ground redevelopment scheme in the early 1990s. It was an event with almost as much significance to the followers of Liverpool FC as the bulldozing of the Kop. Phil Thompson sums up the impact of that sad day: 'It was a piece of history that can never be replaced. It represented so much that was good about Liverpool. When I heard it was gone, a shiver went down my spine.'

*'Thommo' triumphant. In his playing days the Boot Room was usually out of bounds; later it became his office.*

## 'Jesus Christ, son, you look eight feet tall in that. You'll scare the living daylights out of them'

*Bill Shankly to Ron Yeats after introducing Liverpool's new all-red strip*

This writer makes no apology for returning to Bill Shankly again and again. It can never be stressed enough that without him the modern Liverpool, the most dominant force English football has ever known, would not have materialised. Thus his name and his presence will loom forever above all others in the Anfield hall of fame.

Like Matt Busby at Old Trafford, he was the source and the inspiration for everything; and again like Busby - and no one else - he transcended the usual emotions extended towards a football manager by the men, women and children who followed his team.

Of course, there have been other marvellous managers since the war, the likes of Bill Nicholson, Alf Ramsey, Don Revie, Joe Mercer, Brian Clough, George Graham, Alex Ferguson and more. Closer to home, Bob Paisley, Joe Fagan and Kenny Dalglish have scaled incredible heights. All of these men have been respected hugely and held in warm affection; some of them have even been revered.

But for Shanks and Sir Matt, there was something more, something deeper and more fundamental. Ultimately, the feeling towards them could be summed up by only one word: love.

The devotion Bill engendered was a product of so many qualities: the common touch, wicked humour, total honesty; then there were generosity of spirit, the ability to inspire both supporters and players, fierce pride in the club, the list could go on. It all added up to a larger-than-life whole, by turns gleeful, outrageous, friendly and formidable, and it was topped off with the golden knack of winning.

Importantly, he maintained a close affinity with the supporters, was always ready to listen and to talk. Ian Callaghan tells the story of how once Shanks plunged his hand into his pocket to give a stranded Liverpudlian youngster the fare home from a railway station in London. The manager had never seen the boy before and probably would never meet him again, but he saw one of his own in distress and wanted to help. Practically everyone who knew him well has a similar tale to tell.

Bill felt a genuine warmth towards the people of his adopted city. He was moved overwhelmingly by the indomitable good cheer with which so many Scousers accepted the hardship foisted on them by the area's widespread unemployment. The pugnacious yet emotional Scot, who had first-hand experience of lean times in his own childhood, maintained: 'If I wanted a workforce I would pick it from Merseyside and we would wipe the floor with everybody. All they need is to be treated like human beings. The people here have a hard life but they have a big spirit. When they're on your side and all working together, then they take some beating.'

Those who played their own part in the exhilarating process of rebuilding Liverpool FC are unanimous in eulogising the role of the almost evangelically zealous son of an Ayrshire miner. Their recollections of Shankly glow vividly across the years, none more so than those of Ron Yeats, the defensive bulwark of Bill's first successful side and now Liverpool's chief scout.

He speaks of the sky-high standards demanded by the manager of himself and of everyone else at the club. The gospel according to Shanks was that no one should ever be satisfied with what they had achieved; that was in the past. Always they should be striving for a fresh goal, seeking to learn something new every day and to go on getting better. And that applied to the biggest stars as well as the lowliest apprentices.

'The beauty of Shanks was that he made you believe it. He made every player think that he had it in him to achieve greatness. Having instilled that belief, he would then send them out on to the pitch to prove it.'

Undoubtedly, the Reds' messiah was a psychologist and motivator supreme, and he never missed a trick. In November 1964, Liverpool had embarked on their first European Cup campaign with an undemanding 11-1 aggregate romp against the gentlemanly amateurs of Reykjavik. It had been a memorable encounter; the Icelandic hospitality had been magnificent and a good time was had by all, but it was hardly meaningful preparation for the sterner tests that lay ahead.

The first of these was against the Belgian champions, Anderlecht, a strong and skilful side well versed in the rigours of European competition. Shanks recognised the gulf between the two opponents and so sought an extra edge for the second round. Thus it was that for the first leg at Anfield he introduced Liverpool's all-red strip for the first time, after a modelling session involving the mountainously-built Yeats.

Ron casts his mind back to the occasion with an affectionate chuckle: 'One day after training, he asked me to try on this new kit and run out of the tunnel at Anfield while he stood on the pitch to study the effect. He stared hard at me and said "Jesus Christ, son, you look eight feet tall in that. You'll scare the living daylights out of them."'

That was only the start of Bill's efforts to induce a feeling of superiority in his players before they met the Belgians. During the build-up, he declared to his men that Anderlecht were a poor side and could be expected to give Liverpool little trouble. Though unwilling to argue with their eloquent leader when he was in full spate, his charges could scarcely credit what he was saying. A few days earlier they had watched the Belgian international side, which included several Anderlecht men, in action and had been tremendously impressed. The general reaction, though expressed under their breath, was along the lines of 'What the hell is he talking about?'

*Matt Busby, who advised Bill Shankly to stick with Liverpool during his difficult early period at Anfield. Whether United fans would thank Sir Matt for that particular example of his benevolence is open to debate!*

Neverthless, they went out and thrashed their eminent visitors 3-0, and it was then that Shankly came up with one of his most delicious pay-off lines. 'Congratulations,' he told them in the dressing-room after the match, 'you've just beaten one of the finest teams in Europe!' Quite astounding, but utterly typical of the man.

Indeed, it was a regular occurrence for Shankly to watch the cream of the Continent's footballers at the top of their form, then dismiss them in a couple of words, building up his own men all the while. Because of this apparently one-eyed yet actually subtle and discerning ploy, the Liverpool players could never be sure how good the opposition were until they met them on the field. 'Even then,' adds Yeats, 'according to the boss, all our goals were marvellous and all theirs were either flukey or offside!'

Bill's mind games continued to play a massively uplifting part throughout the remainder of a pulsating 1964/65 season. Though the League title was allowed to pass into the temporary custody of Manchester United, the Reds reached the FA Cup Final, where they faced the dour but frighteningly efficient Leeds United, a club destined to be a formidable power in the land and one of Liverpool's deadliest rivals for the foreseeable future.

Clearly Don Revie's men, who had been pipped for the Championship only on goal average, represented a genuine threat, but - at least outwardly - Shanks would have none of it. He told his men: 'You are the best. Leeds are honoured even to be on the same pitch as you. You are going to beat them because you are more skilful, and because you are fitter, and because you are harder.'

Then he went on to declare it unthinkable that Liverpool should let down their fantastic fans, who had paid good money travelling all over the country to watch them. He concluded: 'Because you are the best players and they are the best supporters, there can be only one result. If necessary - and it won't be - you should be prepared to die for them. Now go out and win the Cup.'

It was a masterpiece of over-the-top rhetoric, utterly outrageous but delivered with fervent passion and a straight face, and certainly it didn't hinder the cause. With three minutes of the game gone, the Merseysiders' left-back Gerry Byrne broke his collar-bone but, with his

*Truly formidable: Big Ron Yeats in the all-red strip which Shanks predicted would terrify Continental opposition. It was all to no avail on this occasion, though, with Ron on the point of losing the toss which decided the 1968 European Fairs Cup clash with Atletico Bilbao.*

manager's rousing words still ringing in his ears, he played on. Though the match went to extra time, Leeds were outclassed and Shanks' most cherished dream had come true - Liverpool had won the FA Cup for the first time in their history.

Back at Anfield three days later, the soccer boss who might have made a comfortable living as a 'shrink' was at it again. This time his targets were Inter Milan, billed as the best club side in the world and the Reds' opponents in the semi-final of the European Cup.

Knowing the fans to be in full cry and baying for fresh victims in the wake of the Wembley triumph, he ensured that the multi-talented Italians took the field first. Facchetti, Mazzola et al made the elementary error of heading for the Kop and were greeted by a knee-trembling wall of sound that might have blasted them back down the tunnel. They settled for turning on their heels and heading for the slightly less raucous Anfield Road end.

It was a deft piece of manipulation, but Shanks hadn't finished yet. Next Ron Yeats led out his men and the din was doubled, yet there was still more intimidation in store for the visitors. Bill's crowning stroke, just ahead of kick-off, was to send out Saturday's hero Gerry Byrne, whose fracture had ruled him out of the Milan clash, and wing-half Gordon Milne, who had been unfit for Wembley - and they were holding aloft the FA Cup! Now there was absolute bedlam. The noise took on unimagined dimensions as the two injured warriors set off on a lap of honour, wave after wave of deafening chants reverberating around the stadium like ferocious claps of rolling thunder.

It seemed impossible for the match to live up to such an astonishing demonstration, but somehow it did. Liverpool turned in what was arguably the greatest single performance in all their Continental campaigns to bring Inter to their knees, winning by three goals to one and spurning chances to have doubled the margin. It was a scintillating night, the like of which Anfield had never witnessed before, and while the players had performed superbly, the blue touchpaper for the explosion of emotion which had done so much to lift them had been lit by Shanks.

Sadly, and controversially, the Italians won 3-0 on their own soil to reach the final, but the Merseysiders and their canny manager had learned much from the confrontation that would stand them in excellent stead during future European campaigns.

*Gordon Milne (standing, far left) and Gerry Byrne (next to him) were instrumental in one of Bill Shankly's most devastating mind games on a heady night at Anfield in the spring of 1965 when Inter Milan came calling.*
*Their team mates, standing left to right, are Tommy Lawrence, Willie Stevenson and Chris Lawler; sitting are Ian Callaghan, Roger Hunt, Ron Yeats, Ian St John, Tommy Smith and Peter Thompson.*

*The new manager's confidence and firm resolve are infectious. Nobody can be in his company for more than a few minutes and not realise that here is a rare driving force who will spare himself no pains to get done the job he has in view.*

*The players will find him fair, friendly and always willing to help and advise, but in return he will demand a high price - the last possible ounce of effort each player is able to give.*

LIVERPOOL DAILY POST, 2 December 1959, reporting on Shankly's acceptance of the job.

*Brothers in arms. In fact, Bill Shankly and Bob Paisley, like many people who spent their working lives together, were not particularly close away from the job.*

*Quite a character, this new Liverpool manager, Bill Shankly . . . The thing about him which impacts most on you is his burning zeal for good-class football and for supreme fitness.*

*He . . . will make his players learn to kill a ball and move it all in the same action . . . he will make them practice complete mastery of the ball.*

*If every Anfield fan could talk with Shankly as I did they could not help but be impressed by the sincerity of the man, his enthusiasm and the burning desire to improve the side he joins.*

LIVERPOOL ECHO, 14 December 1959, reporting on Shankly's arrival to take over.

### 'At Liverpool you didn't get injured - you couldn't afford to. If you did... Bill didn't want to know you!'

*Roger Hunt on Shankly's aversion to unfit footballers*

The trial by tumult of Inter Milan was an example of Shankly psychology at its most spectacular, but there were daily, more measured doses for those who worked alongside him. His attitude to injured players, for example, passed into Merseyside football folklore. For Shanks, after an initial brusque inquiry as to their welfare, they barely existed and he spared them hardly a word. He had time only for people who could play for Liverpool and, he conveyed by his attitude, until casualties were fit again they held little interest for him.

Roger Hunt recalls the scenario with a smile: 'At Liverpool you didn't get injured - you couldn't afford to. If you did, it is absolutely true that Bill didn't want to know you! It was rare for him to enter the treatment room. He would just open the door and peer in with a suspicious expression on his face. Probably he would say nothing, or he might make some brief dismissive comment, and then he would be gone.

'Once I remember Tommy Lawrence, our goalkeeper, came into the room limping terribly. There was no suggestion of malingering, which was scarcely likely at Liverpool; he was genuinely hurt and could hardly walk. But he knew the way Shanks reacted to injured players and was worried about the consequences. He talked it over with Bob Paisley, who advised him to bluff Bill by declaring himself fit. That way, Bob reckoned, he couldn't be in the wrong. But when Tommy hobbled up to Shanks and said he was okay, the boss thought he was mad!'

The Scottish goalkeeper, a much underrated performer and a lovely, unassuming man, was acutely embarrassed but it's likely that the shrewd manager knew what was afoot all along. He was an impeccable judge of character and would never have credited that 'The Flying Pig' - as Tommy was known in reference to his ample girth - would have attempted to deceive him.

Indeed, Bill set great store by character, and he had to approve of a player as a man as well as a footballer before he would sign him for Liverpool. Sheer ability was the first criterion, but good temperament, honesty and the willingness to battle were essential, too. Ian Callaghan sums up his former manager's attitude: 'Shanks lived very simply and he had no desire to bring flashy guys to Liverpool. He had a strict set of personal values, which he applied to running the club and to every aspect of life.'

Bill's first wave of signings in the early 1960s included the likes of Preston North End wing-half Gordon Milne, whom he had known from childhood. He had played alongside the boy's father, Jimmy Milne, for the Deepdale club and knew he was getting top value for his £16,000. Then came another wing-half, Willie Stevenson, from Glasgow Rangers for £20,000; centre-forward Ian St John, £37,000 from Motherwell; stopper Ron Yeats from Dundee United for £30,000 and, a little later, £40,000 winger Peter Thompson from Preston.

All these men were of the right type, had proved themselves at their previous clubs and were pitched straight into first-team action. Without exception, they performed magnificently for the Reds, justifying every penny of the outlay.

By decade's end, prices had risen significantly and Shankly, having established the foundation for ongoing success by winning the League twice and the FA Cup once, adopted a cautious and economical strategy in the team-rebuilding process demanded by the ravages of time. He set out to acquire raw talent, usually virtual unknowns from the lower divisions, before the need to replace existing team members was pressing. Then he would educate the newcomers into the Liverpool way of playing and thinking, and only when he was satisfied

*The moment of truth. Bill Shankly announces to the world that he is to quit as manager of Liverpool FC. To say the decision came as a shock, even to those who worked most closely with him, is a massive understatement.*

that they could meet the rigorous Anfield standards would they be promoted to the senior ranks.

In this way he acquired such men as dynamic midfielder cum defender Emlyn Hughes from Blackpool for £65,000, centre-half Larry Lloyd from Bristol Rovers for £50,000, goalkeeper Ray Clemence from Scunthorpe United for just £18,000, utility man Alec Lindsay from Bury for £67,000 and a certain Kevin Keegan, another snip from Scunthorpe for £35,000.

As it turned out, Messrs Hughes and Keegan might have been born to be Reds and needed no 'running in' period, but the rest spent lengthy stints honing their abilities in the Central League side.

This was shrewd husbandry. It removed the potential hazard of paying, say, £100,000-plus for an established star, then having to play him in the first team to justify the outlay, only to find out that he didn't fit. Of course, if they wanted a 'name' player badly enough, they were ready to pay - as they did with strikers Alun Evans (£100,000 from Wolves) and John Toshack (£110,000 from Cardiff City) - and it must be admitted that not all Shankly's dips into the bargain basement were successful.

Winger David Wilson of Preston, Wrexham full-backs Peter Wall and Stuart Mason, even Manchester United's England under-23 forward Phil Chisnall were all cases in point; they were good footballers but didn't have what it took to make the long-term grade at Anfield. However, the theory was sound; if Liverpool had been forced to buy Hughes, Lloyd, Clemence, Lindsay and Keegan in their prime they'd have needed to mortgage their ground to do it!

As it happened, Bill had to break up his first fine team earlier than he had anticipated, then the subsequent period of transition proved longer than he had hoped. In fact, it is frequently forgotten, when reviewing the Reds' golden era, that no major trophy was won between the Championship in 1966 and the League/UEFA Cup double seven years later.

After his retirement, Shanks admitted that his 1960s side had shown signs of wear much more rapidly than he had expected. He believed that a footballer's most effective spell should be between the ages of 28 and 33, as had been the case in his own career. By 28 a player should have learned the game thoroughly and, if he had been truly professional and looked after himself, should be fit enough to put the experience to best use. 'I had bargained for all my players going on until they were 30, at least, but some of them waned a bit and I had to make changes.'

Here was a telling contrast to the twilight years of Matt Busby's superb Manchester United side, the one containing George Best, Denis Law and Bobby Charlton and which, in retrospect, many critics reckon was not broken up early enough. Though more complex factors were involved in the subsequent problems which beset Old Trafford, the two clubs' fortunes in the years that followed offered eloquent testimony to the efficacy of Shankly's brisk assessment of a deteriorating situation. While Liverpool grew ever more powerful, progressing from one triumph to the next, United slid ingloriously from grace, not recovering before spending a season in the Second Division.

Indeed, Ron Yeats felt that his manager's greatest achievement was in *keeping* Liverpool in the top bracket, rather than leading them there in the first place: 'A lot of clubs come up but they don't manage to keep it going. Bill Shankly laid the foundations right, and he made sure everyone at Anfield knew how to carry it on.'

The wisdom of Liverpool's transfer policy extended to buying individuals as all-round footballers rather than necessarily as specialists for any given position. Emlyn Hughes could play anywhere in midfield or at the back, Geoff Strong could play anywhere, period; Alec Lindsay was known as a midfielder when he arrived from Gigg Lane but developed into an England left-back.

Yet perhaps the most vivid illustration of Shankly and company seeing more in a player

*The sheer aerial majesty of John Toshack is captured as the Welshman rises above David Webb (left) and Gary Locke at home to Chelsea in November 1972. The £110,000 acquisition of Toshack showed that Liverpool were ready to part with big money if the right man became available.*

than met most eyes was offered by the case of Ray Kennedy. As a striker, the beefy north-easterner had helped Arsenal win the League and FA Cup double in 1971, but thereafter, surprisingly, his career had lost impetus. Somehow he seemed listless and evidence of a weight problem was there for all to see.

The Anfield boss and his Boot Room back-up team noted this relative decline in a young man whom they believed to have vast untapped potential. Certainly they recognised his marksmanship but saw in his close control, precise distribution and astute reading of the game the makings of an outstanding deep-lying creator.

Accordingly, in what was to be his last major deal before retirement, Bill paid the Gunners £180,000 for Kennedy in the summer of 1974. At first Bob Paisley employed him up front where, without doing badly, he failed to convince in the way that he had alongside John Radford during his early years at Highbury. But then the new manager fell back on 'Plan B', slotting Ray into a left-sided role behind Kevin Keegan and John Toshack. He was a revelation and the most productive phase of his career was under way.

Of course, the loss to Liverpool of Bill Shankly, mentioned so routinely in passing, dumbfounded everyone connected with the club, indeed anyone with the remotest interest in football. Shanks *was* Liverpool and there had not been the slightest hint that he was going to step down. The Reds had just won the FA Cup and were preparing apace, as evidenced by the Kennedy transfer, for a new assault on the Championship in 1974/75.

True, he was 60 years old but he looked as spry as ever, and certainly there had been no noticeable decline in his passion for the game. Yet he announced, using a profoundly moving phrase, that he was 'tired with all the years'.

Later, when the cares of the job were long behind him, there were suspicions that he regretted having made a hasty decision. But still he spoke of being in the game a long time and of management being a supremely arduous task. 'When I arrived at Anfield there was a lot of work to be done. A lot of battles had to be fought. Well, I reached a point where all those battles had been won. I had conquered Everest. I had proved a point to myself and everyone else. I was the manager of a big club; if I wanted to buy a player, or give a player something, then there was no argument.'

In view of Bob Paisley's subsequent phenomenal success, gained in his own right but utilising the resources his predecessor had assembled, there were people who surmised that Bill was envious. Their speculation was fuelled by ill feeling which arose between Shanks and the club over their treatment of him after he left.

But this is not the place to open old and bitter wounds and the man himself, while he talked openly of his perceived hurt, was ready to pay tribute to the achievements of his former lieutenant.

To that end he was asked to speak at the ceremony to install Bob as Manager of the Year in 1977, when Liverpool won the European Cup for the first time and the League Championship for the tenth, being deprived of the FA Cup and a unique treble only by a freak Wembley goal from Manchester United's Jimmy Greenhoff. Bill paid due tribute, but accompanied his gracious words with a loaded remark, delivered as a joke but surely containing more than a grain of truth. He grimaced at his audience and then grated: 'If you think I'm feeling a wee bit jealous - then you're bloody right!'

*Ian Callaghan steps out at Melwood on the road to recovery after an injury. The manager's only problem with the enthusiastic Cally was in getting him to take it gently in training.*

**'I never knew a man sum up a player or a team like Bob.
He would watch a match and have every man's strengths and
weaknesses off pat in a very short time.  It was a fantastic ability '**

*Ian Callaghan on Bob Paisley*

*The hands-on approach. Bob
Paisley was never happier
than when stripped for action
at Melwood, as seen here in
his pre-management days.*

It's monstrously unjust but seemingly inevitable. Somehow, whenever the story of Liverpool FC is told, the most successful manager in the history of English football tends to be under-valued.

Of course, writers dutifully set out Bob Paisley's staggering record of trophy-gathering; they pay tribute to his shrewdness, strength of purpose and unrivalled knowledge of the game; some even refer to the gigantic part he played in the transformation wrought by Bill Shankly. Yet still there remains an inescapable element of 'after the Lord Mayor's Show'.

It's not critical, it's not disrespectful, and in the long run it doesn't matter. After all, Liverpool's amazing achievements under Paisley are enshrined forever in the record books and it's difficult to believe they will ever be equalled, much less outstripped. Nevertheless, talk of Anfield in the 1960s and early 1970s and the name that crops up most commonly is that of the high-profile manager; but let the conversation move on to the years that followed and it is dominated by memories of players, Keegan and Dalglish, Souness and Rush and the rest.

The reason, of course, is the vast gulf in charisma between the two men. Bill was a livewire wisecracking philosopher, a vivid highly-charged character with a beautiful vision and a captivating manner of putting it across. Bob was unobtrusive, solid, seemingly born to be a sideman; he was reluctant to step into the limelight and, initially at least, horribly uneasy when he found himself there.

Bill lived for football and could communicate his heart-and-soul devotion to the game with enchanting word-pictures. Bob was no less committed, no less canny and no less adept at applying his undoubted expertise. Shankly's wit was legendary but there was humour about Paisley, too; it was dry but wickedly piercing, though it did not surface often for public consumption until he had grown in confidence as a manager.

One extremely private occasion when an exquisitely-judged Paisley one-liner had his boss guffawing with delight was on the Wembley bench during the 1965 FA Cup Final against Leeds United. It seems the Leeds officials were congratulating each other on their tactic of denying space to Liverpool's brilliant winger Peter Thompson by deploying their own flankman, the coloured South African Albert Johanneson, in a deep position. One Leeds man observed: 'Thompson's snookered', to which Bob rejoined instantly: 'Aye, behind the black!' It was a gem of which Shanks himself would have been proud, and years later he marvelled at the deadpan manner in which his first lieutenant had produced it amid all the tension of a Wembley final.

From talking to those who played under Bob, a picture emerges of an individual who possessed unrivalled football knowledge but who was a frequently inept communicator, even to them let alone to a detail-greedy outside world which had grown used to a never-ending supply of *bon mots* from his infinitely more colourful predecessor.

Phil Thompson describes Paisley as a unique man of vast insight: 'He knew players and tactics incredibly well, like nobody else. But he was never a great talker and needed Joe Fagan and Ronnie Moran to put his ideas across. They did so brilliantly and it all added up to a wonderful combination.'

Ian Callaghan concurs: 'I never knew a man sum up a player or a team like Bob. He could watch a match and have every man's strengths and weaknesses off pat in a very short time. It was a fantastic ability.'

David Johnson bears witness to the all-seeing Paisley eye: 'He never missed anything in a game. Say you were knackered and thought you'd take a quick breather by tying up a bootlace, he would spot it and tell you about it afterwards. If you suffered a little tweak in your thigh and thought you'd keep it to yourself for fear of losing your place - there was so much talent at Anfield that it was never easy to get back in the team after injury - he would ask you about it.'

'Johnno' marvels, too, at Bob's knack of evaluating a player's potential, no matter how poor a spell he might be having. A case in point was that of Ian Rush during his early days as a Red following his £300,000 transfer from Chester in the spring of 1980. To many observers, the Welshman looked unlikely to make the grade as he struggled to adjust to life at a big club. Paisley, though, recognised something worth encouraging in the rather scrawny rookie, though even he could hardly have visualised the bountiful dividends that would accrue from this particular example of his acumen.

Clearly, he possessed soccer wisdom beyond measure, though memories of his frequently faltering efforts to relate it to others still make David smile: 'He gave some incomprehensible team talks. I shall never forget the first one that Mark Lawrenson attended. As Bob unfolded his plans, the look on Mark's face grew more and more bewildered, and when we walked out at the end he said to us: "What was all that about? I didn't understand a word." We just said "Join the club! It doesn't matter - none of us do."'

Tommy Smith has a fund of stories about Bob's verbal fumbles, but he relates them only after stressing his vast admiration for one of the sharpest brains British football has ever known. Sometimes, he recalls, the manager seemed a trifle nervous as he issued his instructions, never more so than before the first leg of the 1976 UEFA Cup semi-final against Barcelona at the Nou Camp stadium: 'He told us that we had got nothing to worry about, but he was anxious all right. He was so much on edge that he got it muddled in his team talk, telling us at one point that "their left-back is not very fast, but he's quick!"'

Another semi-final, this time of the European Cup two years later, threw up another instance of Paisley's maladroitness as an orator. Seeking to inspire his men as they approached the second leg of their encounter with Borussia Moenchengladbach trailing 2-1, he made much of the fact that several of the Germans were 'old men'. He dismissed 32-year-old Bertie Vogts as past it and reckoned that, at 29, even Rainer Bonhof had seen his best days. What he had conveniently forgotten was that among those he was encouraging were 36-year-old Ian Callaghan and Smithy himself, who was 33. It did no harm, though, giving the players an uproarious laugh, and Liverpool trounced Borussia 3-0 to reach the final.

Alan Kennedy, too, remembers Bob's talks with affection, especially those on the day before a match when tactics were discussed in detail. He admits now what he would never have admitted then: 'We didn't always pay the closest of attention. We were more worried about who would get the chocolate biscuits afterwards and who would have to make do with the plain ones!

'The Boss muttered a bit and had a disconcerting habit of looking at one player while apparently talking to another. Sometimes I wondered what was going on but, luckily, those sessions didn't last very long. If we were puzzled at the end of it all, Joe, Ronnie and Tom Saunders were always there to explain for us. If the manager expressed himself awkwardly, they always knew what he meant.'

In fact, Alan felt a close affinity with fellow north-easterner Paisley, whom he liked and respected immensely. 'Bob bought me from Newcastle in 1978 and I got on with him at once. My mother knew him from the old days in Hetton-le-Hole, a mining town where everybody seemed to know everybody else, and we had a chat about that. It all helped to make me feel settled and comfortable, not under the slightest pressure. Sometimes I felt he was the only man at Anfield whose accent I could understand.

'To me he seemed like an old-fashioned type of dad. He seemed an easy-going, unhurried

*Liverpool's most glittering prize to date, their first European Cup in 1977, provokes an Emlyn-size grin from Kevin Keegan (left) and the genuine article (below).*

man who strolled around with a bit of a swagger, though not in a cocky way - it was just the way he walked. He was never flamboyant and always offered plenty of sound sense.

'I think he was a marvellous man-manager who got the best out of you by building you up. I used to think "I just can't let him down" and if I'd made a mistake in the first half of a game, I'd grit my teeth and somehow try even harder in the second.'

However, despite his rather avuncular image, no one should doubt that Bob Paisley possessed his quota of steel. Certainly he didn't shirk tough decisions - indeed, his ruthlessness in team selection did not endear him to every member of his squad - and even in Shankly's time it was often the faithful number-two who would be the conveyor of unwelcome news. The respect that he had built up in those early years was to stand him in wonderful stead as he progressed towards the pinnacle of his life in football.

*Opposite: A moment of communion. Phil Thompson (left) and Sammy Lee offer the Championship trophy for the Kop's inspection in the spring of 1980. It was the fourth time in five seasons that Bob Paisley had delivered the League crown and, as Thompson said, he was a man of unique gifts.*

*Tommy Smith has some hilarious tales of Bob Paisley's muddled team talks, but he is quick to honour the former Anfield boss as one of the sharpest brains British football has ever known. Here a powerful Smith header puts the Reds in front against Borussia Moenchengladbach in the 1977 European Cup Final, virtually securing what was arguably Bob's most glorious triumph.*

**'Eeeh, what's wrong with you, lad? Eeeh, you'll be okay.
Let's get you outside and we'll soon see what you're like'**

*A typical Bob Paisley approach to an injured footballer - and it worked wonders*

*Bob Paisley in his playing pomp. He was a hard-working wing-half who served the Reds long and faithfully, only to miss out on his moment of glory when unexpectedly dropped from the side for the 1950 FA Cup Final against Arsenal.*

*Opposite above: Bill Shankly - the hardest possible act to follow, but after 13 major trophies in nine seasons, Bob Paisley could say he had made a passable fist of it.*

He was on a hiding to nothing. He was a two-way loser who would be condemned for letting standards slip if he did not emulate his predecessor and for merely winning with another man's team if he did keep the trophies rolling in. He was a buffer manager, a short-term stopgap while Liverpool digested and got over the shock of losing Bill Shankly, their footballing inspiration and spiritual leader.

Such were the greetings extended by various pundits to new boss Bob Paisley when he slipped diffidently, indeed reluctantly, into the Anfield hot seat in the summer of 1974.

But those vulturine observers failed to appreciate two supremely salient factors. Firstly, they didn't do justice to the calibre of the man himself. Secondly, they failed to grasp the startling efficacy of the Reds' deceptively simple, matter-of-fact approach as exemplified by the Boot Room, which would not be threatened by the new regime.

The widely-held view was that the vacancy should be filled either by a proven top-ranker - a Don Revie or a Brian Clough - or that some rising talent with Liverpool connections - maybe Gordon Milne, Ian St John or Ron Yeats - should be given the chance to bed himself in, bolstered by the enormously experienced backroom brigade.

As those closest to him were not surprised to observe, the vast volume of hot air and the miles of newsprint expended on the subject had no discernible effect on Bob Paisley. His reaction to Bill's resignation had been typically self-effacing. First he did his utmost to bring about a change of mind, suggesting to Shanks that he went on a world cruise to recharge his batteries before returning to work. Then, after his honest attempts at persuasion had failed, the erstwhile trainer maintained that he didn't want the top job and that he saw himself only as a stand-in before a new man was appointed.

However, he faced the awesome responsibility of following in the footsteps of a Merseyside deity with characteristic shrewdness and resolution. Realising from the outset that he could never hope to compete with Shanks as an orator or a wit, he simply didn't try. Instead, ever his own man, he announced that he would let his team do the talking for him, though even he could hardly have imagined how eloquently they would hold forth on his behalf.

It would be absurd to deny that Paisley had inherited a collection of top-rate footballers, whose respect he had already earned by his own efforts in helping to lay the bedrock for long-term success. But that was no guarantee of future prosperity. Bob had to prove himself as the man with whom the buck stopped, and at first he had to do so while coping with the potential embarrassment of Shanks continuing to train at Melwood.

Understandably, if a trifle insensitively, the players carried on addressing their former mentor as 'Boss', which must have been excruciating for Bob, although he was at pains to deny his awkwardness. Soon a sense of regrettable unease grew between Shanks and Liverpool, perhaps because the directors were anxious that Bob should not feel suffocated by the charismatic presence of his predecessor, no matter how well-intentioned that presence might be.

As a result - and doubtless there was fault on both sides - Bill stopped using the facilities he had helped to provide and accepted the hospitality of various other clubs. The new manager stressed all along that his own relationship with Bill never broke down, though it's true to say that the two had never been bosom pals away from their work. Whatever the feelings involved, by and large Bill withdrew from the Anfield scene, while Bob got on with his new job.

Though Paisley was hardly a household name, it transpired that the Anfield board had

*Below: Tommy Smith timed his testimonial match perfectly - just a couple of nights after he had scored the crucial goal in the 1977 European Cup Final. Famous faces in the Anfield dugout include, left to right, Steve Heighway, John Toshack, Smithy himself, Jimmy Case, Kevin Keegan, Ray Clemence, David Johnson and David Fairclough. Over a season in which they had also lifted the League title and missed the FA Cup only through a freak goal, these men had done Bob Paisley proud.*

known their man well, their apparently conservative choice proving to be truly inspired. Bob's first term in charge yielded no trophies, but he didn't panic, knowing there was no call for wholesale changes. Instead he tinkered intelligently with his side during that barren 1974/75 campaign, making several unspectacular but enormously shrewd signings - the likes of full-back Phil Neal for £66,000 from Northampton amd midfielder Terry McDermott, a £170,000 acquisition from Newcastle - and giving youth its fling in the shape of locally-born attacking midfielder Jimmy Case.

Thereafter the script entered the realms of what, had anyone ventured to predict it, would have been dismissed as flagrant fantasy. During the remaining eight years of his tenure, Bob Paisley presided over the lifting of no fewer than 13 major prizes - three European Cups, six League Championships, one UEFA Cup and three League Cups - and rebuilt the side along the way. Of the three seasons when Liverpool did not take the First Division title, they finished as runners-up in two and in the remaining one, 1980/81, they came fifth. Oh, what a disaster that season turned out to be - the Reds had to make do with a solitary piece of silverware, a trivial little bauble going under the name of the European Cup!

What manner of man was behind this redefining of the boundaries of soccer success? Like his predecessor, Bob Paisley was a miner's son raised to respect the work ethic. Football was his passion but hopes that it would provide an escape route from life down a pit nosedived when he was 14. After signing the youngster on schoolboy forms, Wolverhampton Wanderers dithered over elevating him to the status of apprentice professional. By then he needed to make a living, so there was no alternative but to go mining in his County Durham hometown of Hetton-le-Hole.

However, Bob was delivered from a life underground when the pit closed and a local builder took him on as a trainee bricklayer. Meanwhile he continued to develop as a speedy, hard-tackling wing-half, his breakthrough coming when he signed for Bishop Auckland, arguably the greatest name in amateur football. While still a teenager he helped the Bishops lift the FA Amateur Cup, then a highly prestigious prize, before signing for Liverpool in May 1939.

Like the rest of his generation, the young Paisley sacrificed six years of his soccer prime to the Second World War. He served in the Royal Artillery, earning the nickname of 'Gunner' while in the Middle East, and took part in the liberation of Rome. Little did he dream on that glorious day, as he rode through the seven hills in a tank, that more than 30 years later he would return to the Eternal City for a momentous celebration of a different kind.

In 1946/47 Bob resumed his career to notable effect, proving his quality in the Liverpool side who became the first post-war Champions. Thereafter until he accepted a job on the coaching staff in 1954, he missed barely a game except when he was injured - with one important, heart-rending exception. After playing in all but one tie as the Reds reached the FA Cup Final in 1950, and scoring in the semi-final victory over Everton, he was omitted from the Wembley line-up to face Arsenal. Manager George Kay believed the more skilful but slower-moving Bill Jones would be more effective than Paisley's non-stop industry, but on the day he was proved wrong, the lively Gunners over-running a rather ponderous Reds midfield.

It was a savage blow to the loyal north-easterner, but one which he accepted with characteristic professionalism, knuckling down to give the Anfield cause four more years of playing service. It was a worthy, often admirable contribution, but one which was to be dwarfed by the monumental achievements that destiny had in store.

In 1954, as Liverpool slipped sadly into the Second Division, Bob Paisley began the second phase of his football life in a manner which, had the doubters of 20 years later taken the trouble to check, might have proved instructive. He took charge of the Reds' reserves, who finished sixth in the Central League in his first season, were runners-up in his second and topped the table in his third. It was the first time the club had lifted that particular title and represented a sizeable achievement, outstripping all the First Division giants, including a

Manchester United team packed with Busby Babes. Clearly, this rookie coach was a man to watch.

Bob continued to impress in typically solid, workmanlike fashion and in August 1959 he replaced the retiring Albert Shelley as trainer to the first team. Come November, manager Phil Taylor succumbed to the strain of his job and resigned, paving the way for the most momentous event in Liverpool's history. The following month Bill Shankly became boss, and Anfield would never be the same again.

Now Paisley was working for a new and vigorous regime of which he became an integral part. Indeed, though Shanks was the prime mover in what was to follow, it would be wrong to underestimate the massive role played by the unassuming north-easterner.

Roger Hunt recalls the trainer making many suggestions on which the manager acted: 'They used to bounce thoughts off each other. Bob was very close to the players in those days, very helpful with encouragement and advice.' Ian Callaghan, too, is in no doubt about the scale of Paisley's input: 'He deserves a huge share of the credit for the success Liverpool enjoyed in the 1960s and early 1970s. That's to take nothing away from Bill, who was the figurehead and motivator and a truly great man. But Bob did so much behind the scenes, including the taking of training and the supervision of injured players.'

Indeed, long before his success as a manager, Paisley had won widespread renown inside the game for his expertise with just about every soccer malady known to man. Certainly in the early days, he might not have been comprehensively versed in medical science, but he could look at a limping footballer and deduce with near-infallibly what was wrong with him.

Tommy Smith, who suffered long and painfully with his knees, would listen to Bob's diagnoses with total faith: 'He would look at your leg and say: "You've done your kneecap, you'll be out for eight weeks." The next day you would see a highly-paid specialist and - surprise, surprise - he would say: "You've done your kneecap and you'll be out for eight weeks!" I always laughed, even when I was in pain. Bob was always one step ahead of the medical experts.'

Paisley himself, a modest man but not falsely so, wrote in his autobiography of his ability to make an instant diagnosis, even from watching an incident on television. He added that others had disagreed with his verdicts, but many times he had been proved right, as when Bill Shankly had doubted him over an injury to Ian Callaghan: 'I remember seeing Ian go down with a bent knee and hurt himself in pre-season training. I saw something from the way he fell . . . I told Bill I thought Cally had done a cartilage, but Bill didn't want to believe me.' Later the player said it was his ankle that was sore and a relieved Shanks said he had known that was the trouble. But: 'Cally played a few games for us at the start of the season, then he had to have a cartilage operation.'

Alan Kennedy remembers Paisley as being more at home with the old remedies than the high-tech innovations that were to become such an important part of treatment: 'Ankle injuries always got the wax bath treatment. It was so hot you could hardly bear it. You wondered if he knew what he was doing but you had to believe him. At least you stopped worrying about your ankle - you'd be wondering how long it would take a grow a new layer of skin!

'Bob's method was based on experience and common sense. When he saw you on the treatment table, he never came out with any complicated theories. He would just wag his head and say: "Eeeh, what's wrong with you, lad? Eeeh, you'll be okay. Let's get you outside and we'll soon see what you're like." It didn't seem scientific, but it worked.'

Actually, of course, Paisley was no witch doctor, having begun learning the rudiments of physiotherapy through a correspondence course during the last two years of his playing career, then going on a full-time course at Liverpool's Belmont Road hospital when he became a trainer. It was a period of sweeping change in the treatment of sporting injuries and the eager student, already well versed in the time-honoured but not always appropriate hot-and-cold-towels method, learned to use the electrical equipment that was swiftly taking over.

It was the sensible way he combined old and new that typified the man, and was an apt example of the down-to-earth outlook that contributed so much to Liverpool's continued success.

It should be stressed, too, that despite his banter with limping footballers, Bob Paisley never expected anyone to play when they were injured. Like Bill Shankly before him, he gave the individual every encouragement to declare himself fit - actually, that's something of an understatement in Shanks' case - but neither man would have risked a player's welfare and, ultimately, his livelihood. It might be fair to say, however, that their views on the pain threshold of the modern footballer were distinctly colourful!

*Party time for Phil Neal and a few thousand admirers after Spurs have been beaten in the final home match of 1981/82 to make Liverpool champions yet again. The Reds have picked up plenty of bargains down the years, but at £66,000 from Northampton Town, the England full-back ranks among the finest.*

**There are a few walks of life in which people drop in to work voluntarily on a Sunday, yet during the season these men made a seven-days-a-week commitment. Quite simply, it was their life.**

*Joe Fagan, a key member of the 'Sunday Morning Club', who gathered in the Boot Room to mull over the events of the previous afternoon. Clearly, to gain admission to that inner circle demanded nothing less than total commitment.*

Bill Shankly had gone, but the Boot Room went on, its importance more marked than ever now that Bob Paisley was manager. The new boss was disinclined to spend too much time in his office, preferring instead the rough-and-ready intimacy of his old 'retreat'.

Sunday morning was a key time for Bob and his trusted inner circle - Joe Fagan, Ronnie Moran and Roy Evans, who had been promoted to coach the reserves in 1974- as they dissected the events of the previous afternoon. There, without fear of interruption in the heart of the silent, empty stadium, they would brew mugs of tea and ponder strategy for the next match.

Paisley described it as a full and frank exchange of views in a leisurely atmosphere, comparing it to popping down to the local. It all sounds extremely cosy, but in reality it was an indication of each individual's total devotion to the cause of Liverpool FC. There are few walks of life in which people drop in to work voluntarily on a sunday, yet during the season these men made a seven-days-a-week commitment. Quite simply, it was their life.

Post-Shankly, the ideals and practices which had brought success remained unchanged, though details were refined as the new manager put his own stamp on the club. Bob was less autocratic than Bill, perhaps paying more heed to the opinions of the players and encouraging more debate; also he allowed them a little more personal licence, the occasional chance during a season to let their hair down. But that was just a matter of personal style. The overall creed, based on simplicity, honesty and taking nothing for granted, was sacrosanct.

Crucially, too, Paisley was as cunning as Shanks, even though his wiles did not attract as much publicity. A telling example cropped up on a pre-season excursion to Germany for a friendly against Kaiserslautern in 1974, shortly after his appointment as manager. Following a wild tackle on Ray Kennedy, the referee was surrounded by outraged Liverpool players and Kevin Keegan was sent off. Appalled by the possibility of his star being suspended, Bob thought on his feet. When the players came off he told midfielder Peter Cormack, who with his dark curly hair was not dissimilar in looks to his more famous team-mate at first glance, that Liverpool were going to plead mistaken identity and that he, Cormack, would be shouldering the blame. They made their case and stuck to the story rigidly, though it all came to nothing as the referee could not attend the London hearing. The Reds' manager, though, had not been willing to take the risk.

He was equally crafty in matters pertaining directly to the game, as Bayern Munich found out to their cost in the second leg of the 1981 European Cup semi-final. During the run-up to the match, a UEFA official began asking questions about the inexperienced Howard Gayle, who was to be one of Liverpool's substitutes. The man's obvious ignorance concerning the fleet-footed flankman made Paisley realise that the ultra-thorough Germans, who would know the rest of the Merseysiders' strengths and weaknesses off by heart, would also know little about Howard. That made him a secret weapon.

Thus, when Kenny Dalglish suffered an early injury, on went the rookie instead of Ian Rush, the more obvious replacement. Howard played a blinder, running amok among Bayern defenders who had no idea what to expect and no answer to his speed and enthusiasm. In the end he, in his turn, was substituted by Jimmy Case when he began retaliating in the face of the rough treatment his bemused opponents had been reduced to meting out. By then, though, Howard had served his purpose and Ray Kennedy's lovely late strike saw the Reds into the final on the away-goals rule. The players had performed admirably, but much of the

credit went to their deep-thinking boss for his recognition of the main chance.

The knack of applying psychology was another priceless attribute Bob shared with Bill Shankly. This was illustrated vividly during 1981/82, when problems with the Anfield pitch - which coincided with installation of an under-soil heating system - had an adverse effect on the Reds' customary home dominance. Paisley was certain the uneven surface was to blame for uneven results, making Liverpool's smoothly skilful passing game difficult to play, and he would have liked to explain this circumstance to the fans. However, he realised that by attaching too much importance publicly to the poor pitch he might have given his players a complex about it. So he bit his tongue, had the bare patches of ground dyed green to improve the appearance and soldiered on, thus not causing a crisis of confidence - and Liverpool duly lifted the title.

Many players benefited individually from Bob's careful attention to psychological detail, one being England goalkeeper Ray Clemence. Undeniably, he was one of the British game's most accomplished custodians since the war, yet still his manager found a way to improve his performance, and in a way that would have escaped a less canny observer.

Ray's one discernible weakness was his goal-kicking, a flaw which he worked assiduously to eradicate but which, occasionally, worried him to the extent that other aspects of his game suffered. He felt particularly vulnerable in wind, which could be unnervingly unpredictable as it swirled around the great bowl of Anfield.

It was Liverpool's custom to fly flags from the top of the Kemlyn Road stand on match days and Bob saw that Ray looked anxious whenever they were fluttering strongly, indicating that the wind was high. Once the manager had identified a possible cause for stress in one of his players, he acted decisively - the flags were removed and the 'keeper's kicking took a turn for the better. Another triumph for psychology and attention to detail.

As the years went by and Bob Paisley piled honour upon honour, he removed every doubt that was ever raised about his capability to follow Bill Shankly, notably in the area of transfers. Some had argued that although he had spent a lifetime in the game, he was not used to the wheeler-dealing involved in signing the right players for his club. That turned out

*'General' Paisley, one of post-war soccer's wiliest campaigners, directs operations from the Wembley bench, while his trusty lieutenants Moran and Evans concentrate on the action.*

to be arrant nonsense as the recruitment of Kenny Dalgish, Graeme Souness, Alan Hansen and many other magnificent footballers was to prove. In fact, he was a master of the market place, not always going for the obvious target, never signing a man whose character he doubted and making precious few mistakes.

Bob was a born winner, first with a team consisting mainly of Shanks' players, then with a side that was completely of his own construction. He never over-complicated his task - believing, like Bill, that many modern coaching methods were absolute twaddle - and ensured that everyone under him performed their tasks simply but well. As he liked to say: 'You can't do the right thing too often.' So basic, but so true.

When he retired in 1983, Brian Clough spoke for the whole of football when he said: 'Bob is a great man, and has once and for all broken the myth that nice guys don't win anything.' Most people who knew him concur with that view, including many to whom he has shown kindnesses both large and small.

One such is Steve Hale, who recalls a morning in Paris when the Liverpool manager came to his rescue. 'It was the day of the 1981 European Cup Final against Real Madrid and, together with another photographer, Frank Loughlin of *The Liverpool Echo*, I had taken a taxi to watch the team train in an out-of-town park. It was in the middle of nowhere and when the session was over we realised we were stranded without transport.

'There was nothing else for it but to start the long trudge back into Paris, but we hadn't gone far when we heard a vehicle pull up behind us. When we looked round, there was Bob Paisley leaning out of the Liverpool team coach. He asked us where our car was and when we said we didn't have one he said "Jump in then, lads."

'It saved us a fearful trek and we were tremendously impressed by his thoughtfulness. After all, he did have a rather pressing engagement at the Parc des Princes later in the day and must have had plenty on his mind.'

Steve goes on: 'He was a lovely fellow who knew his football and knew people, too. He realised which ones were genuine, which ones he could trust. He never raised his voice and always seemed to smile after he spoke - I thought a lot of Bob Paisley.' It was a typical tribute to one of the most widely liked and respected men in the game.

*Howard Gayle, whose shrewd use by Bob Paisley played a significant part in one of Liverpool's most satisfying European victories against Bayern Munich in the 1981 European Cup semi-final.*

*Bob Paisley, that kind and crafty man, emerges from the tunnel at Anfield.*

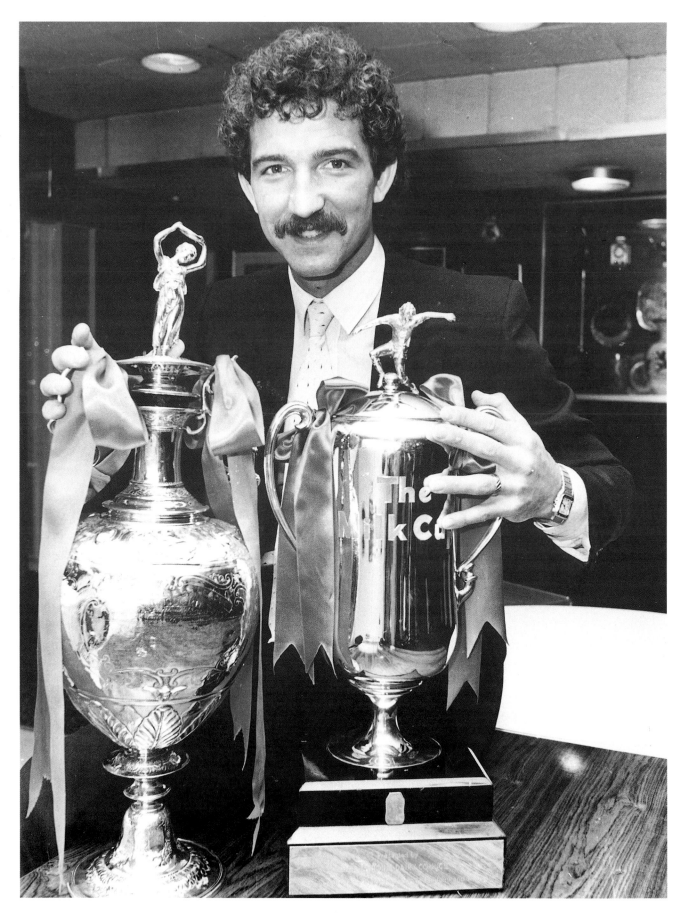

58

> **'He was an unassuming man... everybody's idea of a favourite uncle. But there was no question of taking liberties. He didn't lose his rag often, but when he did... it was frightening'**
>
> *Phil Thompson on Joe Fagan*

No one summed up the ethos of the Boot Room more aptly, more completely, than Joe Fagan. Having been in at the start of the Shankly era, then served as reserve-team trainer, first-team trainer, assistant manager and finally as the boss in a 27-year tenure that did not end until 1985, he spent more hours in the club's homely hub than anyone else. But more importantly, this strong, friendly, understanding man reflected exactly the nature of the institution he served so faithfully. He did so in the way he worked, the way he dealt with people, the very way he lived his life - honestly, simply and utterly free from pretension.

Joe Fagan was born in Liverpool with a deep love of football and it might have been expected that, after impressing Reds boss George Kay in a trial, the enthusiastic young centre-half would sign for his hometown club. But he judged that prospects were brighter some 30 miles down the East Lancs Road, and when he left local amateurs Earlstown Bohemians in 1938, it was to throw in his lot with Manchester City.

The war interrupted the young stopper's progress and it was not until New Year's Day 1947 that he made his League debut, but then cemented his place, playing in every remaining game as City won the Second Division title. Ironically, had he opted for Anfield rather than Maine Road, he might have been celebrating an even more illustrious achievement - that season the League Championship went to Liverpool.

Over the next three campaigns Joe missed only three matches, but could not prevent City slipping back to the second flight in 1950. One year and one broken leg later, he left City to divide his time between the player-management of Lancashire part-timers Nelson and checking for gas leaks in a factory.

He was to make a brief (three-match) return to the Football League with Bradford Park Avenue before taking another step on the managerial ladder by becoming trainer of Rochdale in 1953. At humble Spotland, where his football duties were combined with supervising the laundry and marking the pitches, he served under a promising young boss, name of Harry Catterick. A few years later the two men would be on opposite sides of the great Merseyside soccer divide, Joe as one of Bill Shankly's most trusted aides, Harry across Stanley Park in the Everton hot seat.

It was 1958 when Fagan was recruited to the Reds' cause, moving into a modest house near Anfield that was to remain his home throughout the remainder of his career. He took charge of the reserves, first under Phil Taylor, then for the soccer sage who was to reshape the destiny of the club. Shanks was delighted to find Joe in his backroom team, having tried to sign him for Grimsby Town as a player back in the early 1950s. Now the pragmatic Merseysider proved his mettle, progressing to the first-team coaching set-up in the 1960s and moving up to number-two when Bob Paisley became manager in 1974.

Nine years on, when Bob stepped aside, Joe was handed one of the most intimidating assignments imaginable - following not one soccer legend, but two. As preparations for that 1983/84 campaign got under way, the same sort of doubts that had been provoked by Paisley's accession were being voiced. After all, Joe Fagan was a late starter, having never managed any League club; now, at the age of 62, he was being asked to take charge of one of the world's best.

Charity Shield defeat by Manchester United intensified the speculation, but as soon as the serious business began it became clear that the change of Liverpool leadership had done

*Opposite: Graeme Souness as most Liverpool fans will wish to remember him - as one of the most successful and influential captains the club has known. His recruitment from Middlesbrough ranks as one of Bob Paisley's greatest transfer coups.*

nothing to lessen either the appetite or aptitude for picking up prizes. It should have surprised nobody. Joe understood what was expected; he knew the drill; and he was backed up two kindred spirits in Ronnie Moran and Roy Evans, the latter having stepped up from working with the reserves.

In the event, far from merely consolidating on past success, the new boss actually improved on it! That term, having added to his squad the likes of defender Gary Gillespie (£325,000 from Coventry) and front-runner Michael Robinson (£200,000 from Brighton), Fagan became the first English manager to preside over a treble triumph. The League title trophy, the Milk Cup and, best of all, the European Cup were deposited in the Anfield strongroom to add a further incredible dimension to the Reds' tradition of dominance.

That night in Rome, after Alan Kennedy had clinched victory over AS Roma in a penalty shoot-out, Joe was the focal point of the celebrations. There was no excessive show of emotion but as he sat contentedly among his jubilant players, his dancing eyes and seemingly constant grin radiated both utter satisfaction and a becoming disbelief at the enormity of his achievement.

It was the crowning moment of a career throughout which he had worked conscientiously with precious little public acclaim, but in which he had earned the respect and affection of dozens, even hundreds, of Liverpool footballers. From top stars who played for their countries to apprentices who never made the grade, no one had a bad word for Joe Fagan.

One man who knows him better than most is fellow coach Ronnie Moran, alongside whom he worked for so many years. He says: 'I have known Joe since he arrived from Rochdale and I have always looked up to him. I have never met a nicer, more straightforward fellow. He was what the Boot Room was all about. Just like Bob Paisley, he wasn't interested in the

*Though affable and avuncular for most of the time, Joe Fagan was ready to lay down the law when required. Here he leaps to his feet to issue heartfelt instructions during a derby encounter with Everton. As their expressions reveal, Messrs Moran and Evans recognise the seriousness of the situation.*

fancy side of football, he never looked for the glamour and the glory.'

Moran is adamant that Joe deserved far more recognition than he got. 'He was a marvellous tactician and, it should be remembered, he is still the only manager to win a treble. Some people reckon he did it because he inherited a great team but that's plain codswallop. It should be appreciated more widely that Joe did an enormous amount towards getting that team together and then developing it. He was closely involved in the training, even when Bob was assistant manager. Anything he achieved, he had worked for and deserved. Joe Fagan did a hell of a job for Liverpool.'

Like his predecessors, Joe was a considerable psychologist as Ronnie recalls: 'Sometimes he made a point forcibly to one player, knowing that another was listening. He would know that the one he really wanted to reach would blow up if approached directly, so he got the message across by taking a different route. He knew how to handle individuals according to their personalities; that made him a good manager.'

Phil Thompson remembers Joe as an unassuming man, softly spoken but a good talker, everybody's idea of a favourite uncle. But there was never any question of taking liberties: 'He didn't lose his rag very often, perhaps once or twice in a season, which made it all the more effective when he did. It was frightening then. He was always right though; you knew you were out of order.'

Some players found him easier to relate to than that other quiet man, Bob Paisley, certainly during the latter's term as manager when there was always plenty on his mind. Joe was ever ready to take an individual to one side and to talk over any problem, whether it concerned football or their personal life. That way he engendered tremendous warmth and loyalty from his charges, who also appreciated the clarity of his explanations, something of a contrast to

*Joe Fagan brought massive expertise and experience, as well as that infectious grin, to his new job as manager of Liverpool FC.*

Bob's sometimes enigmatic mutterings.

Joe's wisdom in all matters impressed Alan Kennedy immensely, one piece of Fagan football lore lodging indelibly in the Wearsider's mind. 'He always told me if I was not in possession then I must be in position. He'd say that if I lost the ball then I must get it back, otherwise I'd be letting down ten others who were depending on me. I thought that was an extremely effective method of motivation.

'But he was great with any sort of problem. I remember how he helped David Hodgson, who seemed to be struggling a bit after joining us from Middlesbrough. David was homesick for the north-east and perhaps was trying a bit too hard. Joe said to him: "Do me a favour - go out and have a few beers." He wasn't advocating anything excessive, just a quiet, relaxing drink. So David took the advice and did much better afterwards. It's not the sort of thing that a coach gets credit for, but it's worth so much.'

The combination of steel and compassion was never more evident than when a tough decision had to be made. Kennedy again: 'If he had to drop you, he would put his arm round your shoulders and explain exactly why he was doing it. Then he would reassure you that if you worked hard, you could soon be back in the team.'

One of the first Anfield youngsters to benefit from the Fagan method, back in the late 1950s, was a talented but very green rookie striker called Roger Hunt. He recalls Joe as a hard taskmaster, an old pro who knew all the wrinkles and a smashing fellow whom he trusted implicitly. 'We young players found it hard to put one over on Joe. He impressed us as a firm disciplinarian, yet he was soft-hearted underneath. There was always a suspicion that his bark was worse than his bite.'

When Roger started in the reserves, fresh from success with the British Army team in 1959, he was the only amateur in the side and lacked the fitness of his professional team-mates. 'I remember one game against Preston at Anfield which we needed to win to secure

*Opposite: Roger Hunt, one of many Liverpool stars who owe a debt of gratitude to Joe Fagan. As Roger recalls: 'Joe was a huge influence . . . I could always confide in him or ask him advice.'*

*Sir Roger in his pomp; Hunt scores for Liverpool at White Hart Lane in March, 1964*

talent money. Quickly it became clear that I was struggling to keep up, and at half-time Joe started to say he wanted more from me. But then he saw I was practically on my knees, and he would never persecute someone who was trying their best, so he left it.

'Half-way through the second half I swapped positions with centre-half John Nicholson, but we lost 2-1 and afterwards Joe took me to one side. Without being critical, he spelt out exactly what effort would be needed if I were going to make it in football.' Fagan left the future World Cup hero in no doubt that there was an enormous amount of graft in store - and even then nothing was guaranteed.

'I talked this over with my dad on the way home in the car and he said that maybe I should forget about football as a career. But Joe continued to encourage me and was a huge influence as I went on to reach the first team. I could always confide in him or ask him advice. He was always there and I can never thank him enough.'

Though clearly a serious man when the occasion demanded it, Joe loved a laugh, too, as photographer Steve Hale discovered to his cost on one visit to Melwood. 'I had taken my quota of pictures for the day - there was a good one of Joe in red shirt and black shorts - when he suggested we go for a stroll and a chat. I was wondering what on earth he had in mind, but I found out soon enough.

'We had just passed a group of players when suddenly I felt a terrific bang on the back of my head. One of the Liverpool lads had hammered a ball at me - and Rushie remains the prime suspect. They all split their sides laughing, Joe joining in, and it was obvious that he had led me into an ambush. I booted the ball back in good spirit, even though it had hurt and left me startled. It had been as though he had been testing me, wanting to find out if I could take a joke. Anyway, I never held it against him!'

From these assorted reminiscences, Joe Fagan emerges as a shrewd, caring and humble man, a formidable expert in his field, a person about whom this writer has yet to hear one syllable of criticism. How terribly inappropriate, then, that his working life should end in such horrific circumstances.

His second and final season as manager of Liverpool, 1984/85, finished trophyless, the side weakened significantly by the sale of play-maker Graeme Souness to Sampdoria. But that was as nothing to the circumstances surrounding the last match of the campaign, the European Cup Final against Juventus of Italy at the Heysel stadium in Brussels. This is no place to go into minute detail about the catastrophe which occurred on the sunny evening of May 29; suffice it to say that 39 Italian supporters lost their lives when a wall collapsed following a surge forward by Liverpool fans before the game.

The final went ahead, Liverpool lost to a controversial penalty, but that was irrelevant. The day's true and tragic significance was written across the homely features of Joe Fagan, which were contorted with distress. Tears flowed and he strove to come to terms with the dreadful reality that a sporting contest could provoke such carnage. He had already decided to retire at season's end, though the public announcement had yet to be made.

Duly it was forthcoming and one of soccer's gentlemen walked away from Anfield in despair, overtaken by a calamity which was none of his doing and over which he had no control. To all who knew Joe Fagan, it was a bitter shame.

*Opposite: Ian Rush, who bushwhacked Benfica with a hat-trick on this sodden Anfield night in October 1984, has also been known to lie in wait for unwary photographers, as Steve Hale found out one morning at Melwood. Who set up the ambush? None other than The Boss himself, Joe Fagan!*

**'You might have a nasty cut but it was just a pinprick to him.
"Clean it up with a wire brush", he would advise with a glint in his eye'**

*Tommy Smith remembers Reuben Bennett*

Reuben Bennett remained the least known of the three wise men who became Bill Shankly's lieutenants in December 1959 - he was the only one who didn't go on to become manager - but he was by no means the least vigorous. Though Reuben rejoiced in the title of chief coach, while Bob Paisley and Joe Fagan were first-team and reserve-team trainers, perversely it was Bennett who took charge of physical training.

And what an example he set. Though 46 at the time, there was no exercise in which the teak-tough, sometimes irascible but always good-hearted Scot could not match the players. He echoed Shanks in his passion for fitness, and woe betide the slacker at the back of the pack when he was setting the pace. Not surprisingly, Bill and Reuben became footballing soul-mates, virtually inseparable during their long working hours, even if they didn't always agree.

Shankly considered himself fortunate to find such a kindred spirit *in situ* when he arrived at Anfield, a circumstance which owed much to the canny perception and country-wide connections of club chairman Tom Williams. The Liverpool chief had successfully head-hunted Bennett during 1958 after noting the achievements of the former Hull City, Queen of the South and Dundee goalkeeper since his retirement as a player in 1950.

Reuben, who served in the Army as a physical training instructor, had spent three years as a trainer at Dens Park, then two as manager of Ayr United before coaching Motherwell for a season and then switching to Third Lanark in 1956. During his two terms at Cathkin Park, working alongside Shankly's brother Bob, Reuben had helped to lift the Glaswegians into the top flight, displaying an infectious brand of fiery dynamism in the process. This, Tom Williams decided, was the very man the Reds needed in their campaign to escape from the Second Division and he beat off competition from several other clubs to add him to the Merseysiders'

*The discipline, wit and knowledge of Reuben Bennett (to the far right in the Liverpool dugout) continued to benefit the Reds well into the 1980s. Also looking apprehensive during a tense European Cup encounter with AZ67 Alkmaar in 1981 are, left to right, substitute David Fairclough, Tom Saunders (behind), Ronnie Moran, Roy Evans and Joe Fagan.*

payroll.

Thus Bennett arrived at Anfield in November 1958, watched and digested the somewhat antiquated training system until Christmas and then assumed his duties in January. Life was never to be the same again for the Liverpool players. To some of them, veterans such as the great Billy Liddell and defender Geoff Twentyman, it must have represented a massive culture shock, especially halfway through a season, as rigorous new routines were introduced.

In the old days it was the custom for players to run from Anfield to Melwood on the roads, then make their own way back in their own time. But, especially after Bill Shankly took over, more enlightened methods prevailed. He ordered bussing to Melwood, decreeing that training should take place on grass, and Ronnie Moran recalls Reuben leading cross country runs on the old council farm near Melwood.

'He took us down dirt tracks, had us jumping ditches and pounding across ploughed fields. No one ever knew his age for sure but he never flagged. I have always had a big build and, even when I was playing for Liverpool, I had to train very hard to keep in shape. Luckily I enjoyed it. I knew Reuben would set a good pace on those runs so I used to slot in just behind him and stick with him. Believe me, it wasn't easy.'

Even more impressive testimony to Reuben's rawhide resilience comes from Alan Kennedy, who joined the Reds in 1978 when the astonishing Scot was all of 64 years old. Though he had not been chief coach since 1971, when he had switched to a scouting role, he continued to take the players running.

Alan reminisces fondly: 'Reuben was a fitness fanatic and a fantastic motivator. If we bilked at running around the pitch, he would scoff and say he could do it on his hands. His motto seemed to be "Whatever you can do, I can do better." He wasn't boasting - he just said it to push you into getting the best from yourself.

'Straightness was his watchword. If he thought you had ducked and dived, had not pulled your weight, he would tell you forcibly. He was an incredibly strong man, even when he must have been nearer 70 than 60. If you were larking around and he hit you, albeit in fun, then you'd stay hit. Reuben didn't believe in cosseting softies, either, so you never complained

*One for all and all for one: left to right, Bill Shankly, Bob Paisley, Ronnie Moran, Joe Fagan and Reuben Bennett*

when he was in earshot.'

That latter trait was borne out by Tommy Smith who, following Bennett's death at the age of 75 in December 1989, paid tribute to the former coach: 'He used to say to us: "Get some fire in your bellies. Get out there and get the job done." If you picked up an injury and said you needed treatment, Reuben would look at you and say: "Rub it down with a kipper." You might have a nasty cut, but it was just a pinprick to him. "Clean it up with a wire brush,' he would advise with a glint in his eye.'

*Reuben and the Reds in the Big Apple, May 1964. Having just lifted the League title, Liverpool were guests on the famous Ed Sullivan Show. Back row, left to right: Phil Chisnall, Ian St John, Tommy Smith, Ron Yeats, Bob Paisley, Chris Lawler, Bob Paisley, chairman Tom Williams, Willie Stevenson, Reuben Bennett, Trevor Roberts, Tommy Lawrence, a club official, Phil Ferns and Fred Molyneux. Front row: Alan A'Court, Alf Arrowsmith, Ian Callaghan, Gerry Byrne, host Ed Sullivan, Bobby Graham, Gordon Wallace and Ronnie Moran.*

Another Bennett tradition was stoking the fires of fierce Scottish-English rivalry in the dressing room. Kennedy recalls: 'Reuben always had an excuse after the Scots had lost an international. Either the wrong goalkeeper had been picked, the grass was too long or the ball was out of shape! The banter was wonderful. He took the Mickey a lot but he could take ribbing, too. Everyone had tremendous respect for him. He was a pea from the same pod as Bill Shankly.'

That assessment is echoed by Ian Callaghan, who maintained his friendship with Bennett even after he (Cally) had left the club, the two men meeting to play golf and for the occasional meal. 'Everybody liked Reuben; they loved the bones of him. Shanks and he were especially close. They used to travel in to work together (Reuben never drove) and covered many thousands of miles throughout Britain and Europe to vet opponents before big games. The huge turnout for Reuben's funeral showed how well he was regarded.'

Sadly, Shanks was already gone when Bennett died, so it is appropriate to let the final tribute go to Bob Paisley, who said at the time: 'Reuben was a fine man and no club had a more loyal servant. He was an excellent coach and later in his career he did a lot of scouting for us because he was a very good judge of a player. He could be a difficult man to deal with unless you knew him, but we always got on well. I don't remember ever hearing a bad word about him.'

By the late 1980s he was no longer actively involved, but was still a regular visitor to Anfield. Reuben Bennett could be proud, indeed, of the part he had played in the rise to worldwide eminence of Liverpool FC.

> **'He was possessed by Shanklyism. We learned so much from Ronnie Moran, stuff that we would carry right through our entire football careers'**
>
> *Phil Thompson on one of Liverpool's most influential figures*

Contrary to assorted premature obituaries in the early 1990s, the spirit of Liverpool FC is alive and kicking - and to be found in the ample form of Ronnie Moran. No longer does Shankly prowl the corridors of Anfield and stride Melwood's green acres; now there is no Paisley, no Fagan and no Bennett. But Ronnie is one of that same singular breed, utterly down to earth but infused with an undying passion for the game.

He is unique among the current Reds administration in that he has seen the lot. He shared in the Second Division austerity of the 1950s, he was an accomplished player during the Shankly Revolution, then he coached the men who brought glory after glory to the club during the reigns of Paisley, Fagan and Dalglish.

When Kenny departed so suddenly and unexpectedly, it was Ronnie who held the fort until the new boss arrived. He remained to help steady the ship during the dog days of Souness and, perhaps most important of the lot, he is still passing on his priceless wisdom to the present Liverpool manager, his friend and in many ways his protege, Roy Evans.

Through it all he has maintained a sense of proportion and simple dignity that is second to none, and talks more sense about football than this writer has encountered from any other source in the modern game. Let there be no doubt, Ronnie Moran is special.

*Ronnie Moran, a strapping full-back of the 1950s. At all times, one theme has been constant through thick and thin; whatever Ronnie has done, whoever he has had to upset, it has all been for the good of Liverpool FC.*

The burly Merseysider first donned a Liverpool shirt as a schoolboy in 1949, turning professional and making his senior debut as a full-back in 1952. Three years later he was a regular in a side struggling to regain the top-flight status that had been lost in 1954, and he matured into a much-respected bulwark of the Reds' rearguard. Ronnie was strong and combative, but his play was illuminated by an 'educated' left foot that lifted him well above Second Division standard and he had no trouble in holding his own after Bill Shankly had led the Reds to promotion in 1961/62.

Two seasons later he missed only seven games as Liverpool lifted the League Championship, then enjoyed a spirited swansong in 1964/65, doing well against the brilliant Brazilian winger, Jair, in both European Cup semi-final clashes with mighty Inter Milan. Thereafter he dropped into the reserves, his playing prizes all won, though with plenty of respected judges reckoning he had deserved more international recognition than his two appearances for the Football League. However, that was not the end of the Moran contribution to Liverpool FC. Indeed, it was barely the beginning.

Already Reuben Bennett had recognised Ronnie's leadership potential, sometimes giving him charge of the runners in training, and in April 1966 he got the call that was to shape the remainder of his working life. At the time Joe Fagan was employing him in midfield for the reserves, a suitably central position from which to pass on his vast experience to the youngsters. Ronnie's reaction was typical: 'It was not what I was used to, but I just got on with it. Unknown to me I was being considered for a coaching job.'

The offer came out of the blue while he was waiting in an Anfield corridor to collect tickets for a big League game. 'Bill Shankly asked me to step into his office and he offered me a job. I took it, even though it meant a substantial pay cut. I knew I had little time left as a player, so I had no hesitation.'

That spring he began working with apprentice footballers, continuing as a player-coach during 1966/67 and forming an enterprising combination with ex-Blackpool and England goalkeeper Tony Waiters. Not surprisingly to those who knew him, Ronnie turned out to be a 'natural' in his new role and in late 1967, aged 33, he quit playing to concentrate all his energies on instruction.

There followed steady promotion. In 1971, just before the Reds' FA Cup Final meeting with Arsenal, Reuben Bennett became a scouting spy cum general factotum, Joe Fagan moved up to help Bob Paisley coach the first team and Ronnie took over the reserves, steering them to the Central League Championship at the first attempt. Three years later, when Shankly retired, everyone moved up again and Moran found himself working with the first team, honing the abilities of some of Britain's best-known stars.

Looking back, those illustrious charges are in no doubt about the value of Ronnie's contribution. A typical assessment, and one carrying added weight as it comes from someone who has coached successfully himself, is volunteered by Phil Thompson. Indeed, Liverpool's former captain pays Moran what many would consider to be the ultimate accolade, describing him as 'a Shanks figure in his own way.'

Phil chortles gleefully as he dips into his fund of precious memories: 'To be honest, as a kid I thought he was a moaning git. When I was in the reserves he would hammer away at us and push us all the time to do things the right way. He was going overboard because he believed passionately in what he was doing. It wasn't for me or for him, but for Liverpool FC. He would tell us nicely once, then twice, and then he would come down harder, making people do things the Liverpool way.

'A lot of the boys thought it was personal at the time, but it wasn't. Oh no! It was just that he was possessed by Shanklyism. We learned so much from Ronnie Moran, stuff that we would carry right through our entire football careers.'

Thompson sees his mentor's level-headedness as one of the keys to his longevity and success: 'As soon as any game was over, it was gone forever as far as Ronnie was concerned. Others might have their heads in the clouds over a good result, but never him. He would never rest. Certain other clubs have done well but been unable to sustain success because they got

above themselves at the drop of a hat, strutting and strolling all over the place.

Ronnie would never let anyone get big-headed. He would stamp it out at the first sign. It was always back to basics with him. It didn't matter whether we were playing Manchester United in a vital top-of-the-table clash or Bristol City, who (with all due respect) might have been struggling at the bottom. We had to keep together, give everything, stick to the ethic of collective effort as preached by Bill Shankly. The club owes Ronnie so much. It has taken a long time but now, at last, a lot more people realise his true worth.'

Equally eloquent in his testimony is David Johnson, who likened his relationship with Moran to the one he 'enjoyed' with that uncompromising disciplinarian Tommy Casey during his first spell at Everton. 'I hated Tommy at the time. He gave me extra training, he always seemed to be on my back, sometimes he even goaded me. But all along, unknown to me, he was telling manager Harry Catterick: "This kid's got something."

'Tommy was pushing me to see how I would react. In that way he got me from the youth team to the First Division, and it wasn't until all that had happened that it dawned on me - Tommy Casey's input had all been for my own good! Ronnie was similar. There was never any pleasing him. He was always bollocking people, it was always his voice bawling across Melwood.

'But looking back now, it's plain that he did it all for Liverpool FC. He got the absolute most out of every player. Anyone who shirked was in trouble. He was testing our spirit - he wanted to see if we would come back at him. Every successful club needs someone like Ronnie. I hated him when I was there, but I always wanted to prove him wrong. In retrospect, he was good for us all and he has done a fantastic job down the years.'

Alan Kennedy, too, felt the rough edge of the Moran tongue on occasion, which came as a rude shock after their first meeting. 'Ronnie introduced himself to me when I arrived, said he had been a full-back like me and we had a good chat. I thought "What a nice, pleasant man."

'But very soon he was sorting me out. I crossed swords with him on a few occasions and often I thought he was wrong at the time. But now I realise he was invariably right. And to be fair, if he *was* ever wrong he would hold up his hands and admit it. Ronnie knows football inside out and can always pick the good player from the merely average. He recognises his own men's limitations but makes sure they play to their strengths. At the same time, he knows exactly how to exploit weaknesses in the opposition.'

Kennedy's regard for Moran could hardly be higher: 'In many way he was Mr Liverpool and Bob and Joe respected his views implicitly. He always said exactly what he thought to everybody, no matter who they were. Ronnie was ever ready to offer encouragement, but there were times when we frustrated him and he would get mad. He couldn't lose his hair, though, because he didn't have any!'

Another aspect of the coach's unfussy modus operandi became apparent to Alan after Liverpool won the League in 1978/79, his first campaign as a Red. 'We didn't pick up our medals until the following season and I was expecting a ceremony, some sort of big deal. But it wasn't like that at all. One day Ronnie came into the dressing room with a big box and simply doled the medals out, saying something like "Here's yours, and here's yours, and get a move on because we're off to Melwood in five minutes." And that was it. There was no chance of getting swollen-headed with a man like that.'

Ronnie himself is careful to point out that this attitude did not mean Liverpool were blase about winning things. 'We all enjoyed winning, and when we had won we would always enjoy ourselves that night. But the next day we got straight back to normal. The lads got used to that routine over the years; it was the drill, even going right back to Bill Shankly's day. The only time there was a ceremony was when we came up out of the Second Division.'

That matter-of-fact philosophy manifests itself in Moran's overall approach, both to his work and his life. 'People used to tell me that I had a job forever, but I never thought that. I take it one day at a time because you never know what's round the next corner. How can you talk about next season, even next week, with any certainty? The club has to go on and must always be thinking about tomorrow.'

One thing can be stated with absolute certainty, however, and that is that Ronnie Moran has relished his life in football. 'I wouldn't be in it if I didn't enjoy it. People show their feelings in different ways and I am not one to go overboard - but I *am* still enjoying it. You must want to win, otherwise there's no point in it all, but if you lose then at least you can say you've enjoyed yourself.

'I can switch off at home - my wife makes sure I do. If she sees me staring at the telly with my mind obviously elsewhere, she'll throw a cushion at me. Actually I'm worse when we win than when we lose. I'm lucky that my wife brings me down to earth. She always has done, even when I was playing.'

Since Bob Paisley retired and Joe Fagan became manager in 1983, Ronnie has been chief coach, and he completed the full hand of footballing positions with his beloved Liverpool - player, youth coach, reserve-team coach, first-team coach, chief coach and manager - when he stood in briefly as boss following the departures of Kenny Dalglish in 1991 and Graeme Souness in 1994.

*Good buddies and highly effective workmates: Roy Evans (left) and Ronnie Moran. The former, now manager of Liverpool, has learned so much from working alongside the latter.*

One man who has watched him closely in each successive role has been photographer Steve Hale, and he harbours not the slightest doubt about the debt of gratitude Ronnie Moran is owed by the club.

'The more I hear about Ronnie from those who have worked closely with him, the more I realise what a crucial cog he has been in the Anfield machine. He takes football so seriously, yet still you feel that it is only a game to him. He's been a wonderful bridge between players and management, he's done everything at all levels. His importance to Liverpool has been, and remains, beyond words.' That says it all about Ronnie Moran.

**'Suddenly, five-a-sides were no longer the key to the side's preparation ... there were tales of players going for days without seeing a ball'**

*Reflection on Graeme Souness's controversial changes to Liverpool's training routines*

This book is about what made the Reds special, the laying down of a simple but inspired philosophy, the creation of rock-like foundations which paved the way to unprecedented success. It is about the men who set the standard by which all future Liverpool teams would be judged. It is, in short, about the old way at Anfield.

That way ended, in essence, on the sombre May day in 1985 when Joe Fagan flew home from Brussels a broken man, shattered by the calamity which had overtaken football in general, and Liverpool in particular, in the dark hours leading up to the ill-fated European Cup Final against Juventus in the Heysel stadium.

It is not this writer's brief to examine in detail the vividly contrasting managerial reigns that were to follow, two periods which fall emphatically into the modern era. Even so, certain matters need to be raised to put the past and present in context and, perhaps, point the way to the future.

When Joe Fagan announced his decision to retire, another appointment from within was widely and correctly predicted. No surprise there, then; *that* was reserved for the identity of the new boss. Instead of another graduate from the Boot Room - Ronnie Moran and Roy Evans were the most obvious candidates - Liverpool astounded the football fraternity by giving the job to their star player, Kenny Dalglish. It seems that both Ronnie and Roy had backers in the boardroom, but chairman Sir John Smith favoured Dalglish and, as was customary, he got his way.

There was no doubting the Scot's shrewdness, intelligence or knowledge, but what did boggle numerous minds was the Reds' apparent gamble in consigning their immediate destiny to a man with no managerial experience.

As the record book shows, any concern was monumentally misplaced. While still a player, Kenny presided over the League and FA Cup double in his first season; then he lifted two more Championships and another FA Cup before, apparently, the strain became too much for him and he resigned, with somewhat bizarre abruptness, in February 1991.

By then, though, he had proved himself a truly outstanding manager and demonstrated emphatically that he was his own man, a fact which no one who knew him had ever seen fit to doubt. He was the first Liverpool boss since Bill Shankly not to have served a Boot Room apprenticeship, a factor which manifested itself in his reluctance to spread the vast load of responsibility with his lieutenants. His desire for independence was apparent also in his cool response to the appointment of Bob Paisley in a consulting role, a position he effectively nullified by seeking the opinion of the former chief only rarely.

Further evidence that he, and he alone, made the crucial decisions came with his sacking of Geoff Twentyman, the club's hugely successful chief scout since 1967, and Chris Lawler, who had guided the reserves to two Central League titles and one runners-up spot in the three terms since Joe Fagan hired him as a coach in 1983. Both men were highly respected former Liverpool players and their enforced departures just a year into Kenny's reign caused shock waves through a club that had seen no backroom dismissals in more than a quarter of a century.

However, Dalglish was far too canny to dismantle wholly a system that had achieved so much over so many years. Thus, while not spending long hours in the Boot Room himself, he was content for Messrs Moran, Evans, Thompson and youth development officer Tom Saunders to keep alive that unique institution. Crucially, too, five-a-side games continued at the heart of the training routine, and the club duly prospered.

*Graeme Souness on the Kop the day after taking over as manager. His popularity was destined to plummet dramatically among many of those who spent their time and their money on that most famous of terraces. He spent £21.45 million on transfer fees (of which £12.325 million was recouped) but never captured the hearts of the people.*

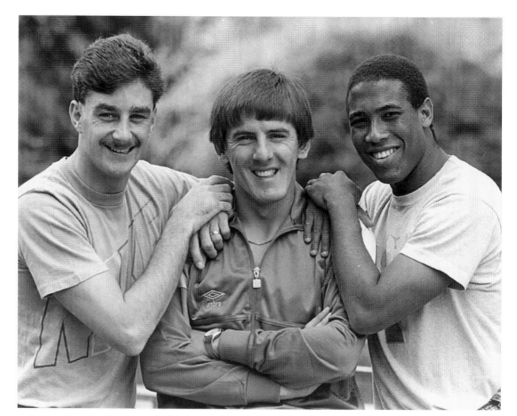

Of course, by the time of his dramatic resignation, when apparently he was so wound up with stress that those closest to him feared for his health, Kenny had lived through the incalculable trauma of the 1989 Hillsborough disaster, which had cost the lives of so many Liverpool supporters. As well as carrying the footballing fate of one of the world's leading clubs on his slim shoulders, he had emerged as a leader both caring and sensitive, dignified and humane, winning widespread praise for his handling of a city's grief.

Publicly, at least, this most private of men appeared to come through the ordeal unscathed, leading the Reds to the Championship in 1990, yet who can say what a personal toll was exacted? It was at a time, too, when his team was in need of some radical rebuilding, a mammoth challenge even under less trying circumstances. In retrospect, then, it seems entirely understandable that he could no longer cope, albeit temporarily, with the at-times hysterical demands of an increasingly pressurised profession.

And so to Graeme Souness, who replaced his countryman after seven weeks of Ronnie Moran's faithful stewardship had kept the Reds in contention for a title that would eventually slip away to Arsenal. Here was another strong man, much more overtly so than Dalglish, an individual renowned for his ruthlessness both as a player at Anfield and elsewhere and as manager of Glasgow Rangers.

We will not dwell for long on the details of his 33 months at the Anfield helm, which were excruciatingly painful both for Souness himself and for everyone who holds Liverpool dear. Suffice it to say that where Kenny was content to let the Boot Room philosophy continue as a tried-and-tested buttress for his own new ideas, Graeme was out to impose a wholly new order.

True, the trusted retainers Moran and Evans remained at the club and continued to give their all for the new manager. But there was a new face at the top of the backroom pecking order, that of ex-Liverpool player Phil Boersma, a Middlesbrough team-mate of Souness in the 1970s who had since worked under him as physio-coach at Ibrox. The influence of the old guard was in decline.

Suddenly, five-a-sides were no longer the key to the side's preparation. Indeed, there were

tales that the players could go for days without seeing a ball, and that when they did they would be forced to practise laborious set-piece routines that bored them rigid. Former Reds shook their heads in disbelief and muttered about sacrilege, while there were well-publicised differences of opinion between Souness and senior players such as Ian Rush, Bruce Grobbelaar and John Barnes.

A further, far-reaching change was the controversial decision to stop bussing the players from Anfield to Melwood for training, the system introduced by Shankly and followed thereafter by Paisley, Fagan and Dalglish. Now the players reported individually to the training ground by car and all the benefits of the old routine - less injuries, more camaraderie etc - disappeared. Of course, it's impossible to prove that the appalling fitness problems the Reds suffered during the Souness regime - and to which he was wont to refer when taxed on his team's poor performances - were attributable to the change, but the implication is clear. Some £300,000 was spent on upgrading Melwood to facilitate this particular aspect of the revolution, and there is no shortage of people close to the club who reckon it could have been far better spent.

Though Liverpool did manage to win the FA Cup in 1992, none but the most rabid Kopite would claim the triumph was a glorious one - the Reds were twice outplayed in the semi-final by gallant underdogs Portsmouth, who succumbed only in a penalty shoot-out - and by the time Graeme resigned in January 1994 his public credibility was virtually nil.

Expensive new players had not fitted in, nearly three seasons had passed without a meaningful challenge for the League title and cup encounters with lower division teams had become occasions to fear - as anyone who attended the embarrassing meetings with Bolton, Bristol City, Peterborough and Chesterfield would bear witness. Team spirit was demonstrably low, and whether he had bought badly, or bought well and managed badly, the upshot was the same.

Graeme's professional disaster had coincided with a series of personal misfortunes - notably a heart condition which had necessitated a triple-bypass operation - and the day he left Anfield for the last time as manager he cut a sad and sorry figure. The fans had turned against him with a vengeance and, as ever in such cases, he carried the can for events which were none of his doing.

Of course, ground redevelopment to turn Anfield into an all-seater stadium, involving the demolition of both the Kop and the Boot Room, would have been carried out whoever was manager. But the disappearance of these two symbols of success and continuity became linked inextricably, if illogically, in the public mind with the team's travails and poor Graeme took much of the flak. Scouse humour, ever irrepressible through the lean years as well as the fat, even had it that the famous little bunker just had to go - because it was too small for the Souness ego!

Truly, with Everton also bumping along the bottom of a debilitating trough, Merseyside soccer was at a low ebb; there was even talk that, come the new season, the resurgent Tranmere Rovers might be the only local club in the Premiership.

However, for all those who prized the old Liverpool way, the Boot Room way, there was heartening news in February 1994. Roy Evans was appointed manager of Liverpool FC.

*The almost surreal scene at Anfield in the aftermath of the Hillsborough disaster. It was a situation which Kenny Dalglish handled with the utmost dignity and humanity, but at what personal cost in terms of stress, none but he and his family can say.*

**'Neither pushy in enforcing his authority, nor a push-over
for those who might confront it... he is an accessible personality,
a figure to whom the fan on the street can relate with ease'**

*Thoughts on the appointment of Roy Evans as manager.*

ew people took much notice at the time; the talk was all of Shankly's resignation and Paisley's promotion. But on the day in 1974 when 25-year-old Roy Evans was elevated from the poignantly plentiful ranks of footballers who would never quite make the top grade to become Liverpool's reserve-team coach, club chairman Sir John Smith made a startling prediction. He announced: 'We have not made an appointment for the present, but for the future. One day Roy Evans will be our manager.'

Those who pondered on that incongruously portentous proclamation, and they could not have been many, might have been excused for dismissing Sir John's words as wishful thinking, or even as well-meaning but fanciful encouragement for a youngster embarking on a demanding new career. But the Reds' chairman was not a man given to flights of fancy; he had meant what he said and, some 20 years on, his bold prophecy proved to be correct. In the wake of the Souness debacle, on January 31 1994, Roy Evans became manager of Liverpool FC.

It was a welcome return to Boot Room rule. That cherished symbol of all that was best about the club might have perished physically, but everything it stood for was preserved in the person of the new boss. Roy had lived for Liverpool from the fateful mid-1950s afternoon when he had left his home in Bootle with his older brother Malcolm, boarded a number-68 bus to Stanley Park and walked into Anfield to watch his first big-time football match. He was seven then, just old enough to begin a lifelong love affair with the Reds.

In the years that followed he stood on the Kop week in and week out, relishing the exploits of Bill Shankly's first great side, packed with heroes like Roger Hunt, Ian St John and Ron Yeats. As he grew up, Roy enjoyed heartening success as a player, emerging as a skilful, if rather one-paced left-back. He played for England Boys and did well, moving his manager, that splendid judge of character Tom Saunders - himself destined to become a key member of the Anfield Boot Room brigade as youth development officer in the 1970s and 1980s - to describe him as having a heart the size of a lion's. And, glory of glories, Roy became a professional with Liverpool.

All too soon, though, that momentum evaporated. Although he reached the fringe of the senior squad, and made 11 first-team appearances in the early 1970s, it became apparent that he was never going to hold down a regular place. It seemed he faced an unappetising choice between lingering at Anfield as an eternal reserve and playing out his career at a lower level.

But those who had guided his professional progress since boyhood, the likes of Bill Shankly and Bob Paisley, had seen something special in the make-up of the unassuming but unwaveringly enthusiastic Merseysider. They had watched him with his peers and with younger players and had recognised the makings of a successful coach. Ronnie Moran had just stepped up to help with the first team and someone was needed to take over the reserves; Paisley identified Roy as that someone and offered him the job.

Now came an agonising decision for the young man. He had always dreamed of playing for his beloved Liverpool and, at 25, he was understandably reluctant to admit that he was not good enough. He informed his manager that he wanted to play, not coach, but Bob was persistent, spelling out the stark truth about his footballing capabilities and repeating the same offer three or four times. In the end, after protracted soul-searching and much encouragement from such as Joe Fagan, Ronnie Moran and Tommy Smith, Evans took the

*Opposite: The man most likely to . . . Roy Evans during his long and thorough apprenticeship for Anfield's top job.*

*Sir John Smith, the Liverpool chairman whose startling prediction for the future of Roy Evans came true.*

*Two of the finest role-models any prospective soccer boss could wish for: Bob Paisley and Bill Shankly, from whom Roy Evans picked up enough football lore to fill any number of those Boot Room notebooks.*

clear-headed option of remaining with the Reds in a new and potentially fulfilling capacity.

Of course, it was something of a gamble, but any doubts about Roy's capabilities were quick to disappear. Though possessing no official coaching qualifications, he was blessed with a lively mind and proved adept at communicating with the youngsters in his charge; and while he was the most amiable of men, he could exhibit steel at need, finding no problem in instilling discipline as well as soccer expertise. The upshot was that Liverpool reserves won the Central League in each of Roy's first three seasons at the helm, going on to enjoy almost non-stop success before he moved up to help Ronnie Moran with the seniors when Joe Fagan became manager in 1983.

Ronnie, who played an enormous personal part in Roy's Boot Room education, sums up his regard for his one-time protege, now his boss, in one succinct sentence: 'He was always the right sort of lad, we never had the slightest doubt about him.'

Though his merits as psychologist, diplomat and father confessor have undoubtedly proved valuable to countless household names over numerous campaigns, Roy himself describes his input in characteristically modest terms: 'If the players were on cloud nine, then we (the coaches) made sure we weren't. If they were a bit down, then we would be chipper. That way we maintained the right balance.'

He believes that the Boot Room's sense of continuity helped, too. He stressed every manager's need for loyalty and solidity from their staff, adding significantly: 'But these men have not got to be subservient. They have to state their case. No club needs yes-men, they can't afford them.'

A further illuminating insight into the rise of Evans the Coach comes from David Johnson, who came under his aegis during the England centre-forward's periodic sojourns in the 'stiffs'. David recalls: 'Roy always had a lovely manner about him. You could go to him and talk about anything, and when he spoke you listened. Obviously he was marvellous with the youngsters, but he also did a lot for older players. They might be swearing and annoyed at being dropped from the first team but, almost invariably, Roy could calm them down with a

few quiet words.

'He had the ability to harness people's understandable frustration for the good of the club, beguiling the best out of them. Certainly he helped to keep me ticking over on occasions. I was tremendously impressed by his man-management skills, and also by his knowledge of football. He could get people to play the right way, the way Liverpool expected. Overall, Roy did a great job.'

Having switched his area of operation from Central League to First Division, Roy continued to make a favourable impression and the conviction grew among close observers that he was top management material. His name was thrust forward in 1985, and again in 1991, but first Kenny Dalglish and then Graeme Souness received the call.

When Souness brought in Phil Boersma as his right-hand man, it seemed that Evans' influence had decreased hugely, perhaps terminally. But that all changed in May 1993 when Roy was made number-two to a chastened Souness, who had been expected to leave there and then, but survived thanks largely to the support of his friend, chairman David Moores. In fact, Graeme hung on for another eight harrowing months before stepping down and, at long last, Roy's hour had come.

In announcing the appointment of his club's 14th full-time manager, Moores described Evans as 'the last of the Shankly lads,' an accurate and telling description. Having spent so much time in the Boot Room he had learned his trade from the best, and learned it thoroughly, knowing the club at every level.

It was an emotional moment for Roy, who told his inaugural press conference: 'Liverpool FC has been built on a sense of pride. I felt that pride when I first came to Anfield and it has lived with me throughout my time here. It's very much with me today as I am appointed manager.' He revealed that when offered the job, it took him all of two seconds to think about it before accepting it. He recognised that restoring the Reds to their rightful position at the top constituted a massive responsibility, but there had been not the slightest possibility of

*David Moores, the Liverpool chairman who backed his friend Graeme Souness to the hilt, but eventually had to accept his resignation.*

*Roy Evans takes the first team squad on his first morning as manager.*

*Robbie Fowler, who came through the Liverpool system under the canny guidance of Phil Thompson. The full potential of this young man beggars description.*

shrinking from it.

The football world was united in its affection for the engaging Evans, who accepted a contract that runs until midway through 1996. But one question seemed to be on everybody's lips - was he tough enough for such a formidable task? Those who knew him well insisted that there would not be a problem. Though he was renowned for the gentle touch, for lending a sympathetic ear to egos bruised by the high-level ranting of Ronnie Moran, there was no questioning his inner strength.

Early evidence that Roy could take tough decisions came with the axing of highly-priced defenders Mark Wright and Julian Dicks after their poor showing in a friendly against First Division Bolton Wanderers during his first pre-season preparation as boss. Openly and firmly, he explained his reasons - Wright's attitude and Dicks' lack of fitness - and made it devastatingly clear that any player who took liberties did so at his peril.

Yet here was a man who enjoyed sharing the occasional beer with the footballers in his charge, who was ready to enjoy a joke with them and who acted, in every way, like a civilised human being. Neither pushy in enforcing his authority, nor a pushover for those who might confront it, Roy offered a striking contrast to his two most recent predecessors. There was none of the obsessive privacy of Dalglish or the driven intensity of Souness; in their place was

*Steve McManaman, whose ebullient form at the outset of 1994/95 has raised hopes of a Reds renaissance.*

a more accessible personality, a figure to whom the fan in the street could relate with ease.

Exemplifying his reasonable approach, Roy wasted little time in introducing weekly players' meetings, at which all ideas could be pooled. Instead of fearing so-called player-power, he sought to harness it, feeling it foolish not to tap such a rich pool of experience.

One of the most senior Reds, Ian Rush, voiced the general opinion of his team-mates when he said: 'Roy knows the players and gets on with them, as well as knowing how to get the best out of them. He IS a nice guy, but as a manager you can't be nice all the time. I'm sure that, like Bob Paisley, he'll know where to cut the tape.'

All splendidly positive stuff but, that said, Roy still has to produce results, and although Anfield expectations are not as high as in recent decades, he neither expects nor desires a lengthy 'honeymoon'. The early indications were that he wouldn't need one, the Reds beginning 1994/95 with a thrilling sequence of victories, projecting a sense of purpose and team spirit that had been absent for too long. Roy had plenty to prove; for instance, his acumen in the transfer market had yet to be tested thoroughly, though the purchase of classy centre-backs Phil Babb and John Scales augers well. But, to the undisguised joy of supporters driven to distraction by Souness, prospects were healthier than at any time since the club's last Championship success back in 1990.

And two things were certain. First, after working for 30 years to earn his chance in the top job, the new boss would not be relinquishing it lightly. Second, though football has changed and the world has moved on, Liverpool under Roy Evans will adhere to the timeless principles of Shanklyism. What could be more reassuring?

*Roy Evans introduces new signing John Scales to Anfield. The purchase of the Wimbledon centrte-half, alongside that of Coventry defender Phil Babb, indicated that Evans was interested only in recruits of the highest quality.*

## 'He had a great presence about him, a natural authority... we listened to him intently and we learned so much from him'

*Alan Kennedy on Tom Saunders*

*Tom Saunders, whose sagacity and enthusiasm has been a major but not widely publicised factor in Liverpool's long-lasting success.*

One of the most influential, yet widely unsung members of the Liverpool Boot Room brigade was not part of the managerial hierarchy, nor even employed by the club as a coach. The name: Tom Saunders, as astute a judge of footballers and, equally important, of people as anyone at Anfield during the last quarter of a century.

A former headmaster, Tom ran the Liverpool and England Schoolboys teams in the 1960s before joining the Reds as youth development officer in 1970. That remained his title for some 16 years, though his contribution to the cause was not restricted to supervising his conveyor belt of young talent.

In such esteem was the articulate Saunders held by Bill Shankly, Bob Paisley *et al* that they trusted him to both vet future opposition and scout for possible signings. On those missions - sometimes in company with the manager, at others with Reuben Bennett - Tom travelled all over Britain and Europe.

He was an avid student of the Continental game in particular, and Ronnie Moran pays a heartfelt tribute to his expertise: 'The input of Tom Saunders played an important part in Liverpool's European success. He has a wonderful ability to assess a team's strengths and weaknesses, then communicate that knowledge to the manager and coaches.'

Tom, who retired as youth development officer in 1986 but continued to serve the club and has been a director since 1993, is held in the highest esteem throughout the Anfield organisation. In boardroom, dressing room, tea room - and certainly in the Boot Room before it was pulled down - he has been accorded universal respect.

Alan Kennedy encapsulates the players' attitude towards a man who was no more than a semi-professional footballer himself - he finished his career across the Mersey with New Brighton - but whose understanding of the game and its demands was so comprehensive.

'He had a great presence about him, a natural authority which I suppose carried over from his days as a headmaster. He was a very strong character yet he never sought to knock people down, never seemed to get angry.

'He was always on the bus when we travelled to Melwood and was full of stories about the old days. We listened to him intently and learned so much from him. Tom Saunders was a truly great communicator and must have been a great help to Ronnie Moran and the other coaches. Bob Paisley, in particular, attached great weight to his views on foreign opposition - and the results speak for themselves.'

Later Tom was a confidante and aide of Kenny Dalglish, not a man to invest his trust lightly, and their close relationship speaks volumes for the stature of the older man.

As he has a knack of doing, Ian Callaghan sums up neatly: 'Tom's recruitment was a massive plus for Liverpool. He was clever, yet as down-to-earth as the rest of the regime and a marvellous ambassador. He was exactly what the club needed.'

Of course, what any club needs as well as outstanding personalities such as Tom Saunders is strength in depth at all levels, and Liverpool had a habit of recruiting the right men from their own 'family'. Apart from Bob Paisley, Ronnie Moran, Roy Evans and Kenny Dalglish, many other former Reds have given sterling service to the club after their playing careers were over.

Following Evans in charge of the reserves have been Chris Lawler (1983-86), Phil Thompson (1986-92) and Sammy Lee (1992 onwards), three of Liverpool's finest and England internationals all. Lawler didn't put a foot wrong in his coaching work and had even

*Opposite: 'This is Anfield' says the sign, expressing a sentiment that will never cease to be special.*

84

been mentioned as a possible successor to Joe Fagan as manager in 1985, only to be dismissed surprisingly by Dalglish a year later. Thompson, too, did a magnificent job, his native humour, common sense and wide knowledge of the game benefiting Liverpool's young bloods for six years before Souness saw fit to sack him.

Lee has picked up where his fellow Merseysider left off and offers much promise for the future. Meanwhile, a steady supply of raw material for Sammy to mould is ensured by Steve Heighway, who as youth development officer is carrying on the splendid work of Tom Saunders.

Still in the realm of talent-spotting, Ron Yeats - Shanks' colossus in the 1960s - has been chief scout since 1986, when he was appointed by Dalglish to replace Geoff Twentyman, another former Anfield centre-half. Geoff, a stalwart of Liverpool sides in the 1950s, had headed the club's scouting operation since 1967, but was judged surplus to requirements by Kenny. Ironically enough, he went on to work for Graeme Souness at Glasgow Rangers.

Yet another ex-Red who has returned to his spiritual home is Doug Livermore, who played a handful of games in midfield as Shankly was breaking up his first fine team in the late 1960s. Most of his outings, though, were alongside Roy Evans in the reserves, and it was Roy who brought him back to Anfield to share first-team duties with Ronnie Moran in August 1994.

Scouser Doug, whose lugubrious countenance belies a wicked sense of humour, had proved himself an outstanding coach at Cardiff City, Swansea City, Norwich City and, most notably, during a spell in charge of Tottenham Hotspur. Also, he has served as assistant manager of Wales, and his experience and imagination constitute a shrewd addition to the already-rich array of coaching talent in place at Anfield.

*Shanks in his element, among the fans who loved him - and the feeling was mutual.*

Finally, a mention for John Bennison, who worked closely with Tom Saunders to hone the talents of the club's youngsters for more than 20 years. Liverpudlian John, who retired in 1993, never played for the Reds or any other professional team, but there was nothing amateur about his contribution. Yet another quiet man, he earned the total respect of those he worked with - and bearing in mind the identity of his colleagues, that is some achievement.

## 'If you take one straw on it's own, then it is easy to snap it. But put a hundred together and they are unbreakable'

*David Johnson on Liverpool's so-called secret*

*David Johnson in his Liverpool heyday.*

And so to the most tantalising, agonised-over question in football - what is the Liverpool secret? What has set them apart from other clubs, who have known fleeting success only for it to fade away while the Anfield Reds have marched on from one triumph to the next?

Down the decades, that mystery has exercised the game's finest minds. Legion are the managers and coaches who have quested in vain for some illusory method, or formula, or *something*, that would explain Liverpool's unrivalled supremacy. Some, after much deliberation, have simply given up the problem with a rueful shake of the head; others have considered complicated tactical theories before admitting defeat; still more, lost in admiring bewilderment, have ascribed to Shankly and Co the powers of footballing witch doctors, men who could tap some basic earth-force beyond the reach of ordinary mortals!

All good fun, and those who have served the club join in, before explaining that, of course, there is no secret as such . . . and they are telling the truth. But there *are* good reasons for the Reds' quarter-century of dominance. They are crystal clear, rooted in humility and nurtured by the best values in life.

Over to David Johnson: 'Every manager and trainer, no matter how famous, has wondered about the Liverpool secret. Many of them thought they could go into the Boot Room and maybe pick up the method. When I went back to Everton for a second spell in 1982, Howard Kendall asked me what the secret was.

'I told him: "If you take one straw on its own, then it's easy to snap it. But put a hundred together and they are unbreakable, they gain strength from each other. Similarly, offer one reason why Liverpool were great and it might not seem like much; but put all your reasons together and you have the so-called secret."

'At Anfield, the tiniest details received minute attention. The simple things were done well. Liverpool never allowed the small things to go wrong and the big things took care of themselves. Meanwhile, everybody kept their feet on the ground.'

It sounds too basic to be true, and David recalls that Kendall was sceptical, but other former Reds offer variations on the same theme. Ian Callaghan is especially persuasive: 'It was always drummed into us that whatever we won counted for nothing the next season. It was just another season and we had to start work all over again. Nobody could get too big for their boots. The coaching staff would always crack down heavily on the merest hint of big-headedness, and so would the other players, especially Smithy. He would say forcibly that we were all earning our wages for each other, and that no one did it on his own. I don't recall anyone arguing the point.'

That attitude is reinforced by Ronnie Moran, who maintains that if a club has people who can play the game and who have the right character, then provided they remain level-headed the rest will follow. Always he is amazed by the disproportionate joy of some opponents should they happen to beat Liverpool. He has watched players celebrating a single win as though they had won the pools and seen a chairman pop champagne corks for no more than an early-season League triumph.

'I asked him: "What's the point of celebrating like that over one result? The end of the season is a long way off." He replied "Ah, but we've beaten Liverpool" as if they deserved a trophy for that alone. Of course, they lost their next match, and that chairman's reaction after the game with us might be part of the reason why.'

Ronnie's creed is that any team is only as good as the last result. He never allows players

Opposite: A night to remember for David Johnson, who had just helped Liverpool beat Real Madrid to lift the 1981 European Cup. 'Johnno', an acute observer of the Merseyside soccer scene, is both eloquent and persuasive when he talks of Liverpool's so-called secret.

to bask in the glory of past achievements, no matter what their import. 'We don't even dwell on the last match, let alone the last season. Keeping an even keel and looking ahead, that's all that matters.'

It's an approach which new boss Roy Evans is delighted to espouse. He calls it instilling a sense of reality, and knows he couldn't have a better man than Moran to enforce it. 'I remember when the players were on a high about a club trip to South Africa, looking forward to all the sunshine. But Ronnie just broke in and told them that it wouldn't be long before they would be lapping Melwood again. That stopped them getting carried away!'

Not that Liverpool players are treated like children. Quite the opposite, in fact, which Alan Kennedy believes is another vital facet of the club's success. 'At Anfield they always treated us like men, never belittled us. If we were honest with the staff then they would be honest with us - what more could anyone ask?'

Also Alan reckoned that introducing new talent every summer, no matter what had been won they previous term, was a shrewd policy which kept everyone on their toes. 'After I scored the winner to beat Real Madrid in the 1981 European Cup Final, I thought I was safe for a bit. I'd been at Anfield for three years, we had won a few trophies and I reckoned I'd cracked it. But that close-season they bought Mark Lawrenson and put him in my position. That made me try even harder to get my place back - and I did. No one can afford to relax at Liverpool and the club benefits.'

Kennedy attributes the existence of such sound working practices to the magical chemistry between three men who came together at Anfield more than 30 years ago. Sharing the load, manager Bill Shankly, chairman Sir John Smith and secretary Peter Robinson had ensured that every aspect of club life was handled correctly. They laid the ground rules and Liverpool FC took off.

Steve Hale, who has covered the whole incredible story, believes that the quest for the Reds' secret will go on forever, no matter how many logical explanations are advanced by the people most imtimately involved. 'Common sense tells me that there was never any secret; that it was just a matter of fine footballers playing the beautiful game, and of honest men who loved their work preparing them for it in the most simple, humble and thorough manner possible.

'And yet, there is just that little seed of doubt that maybe there *was* some formula that was so secret it was known to only four or five people. But no, it couldn't be . . . could it?'

# MANAGERS' LOG

**BILL SHANKLY** Born: Glenbuck, Ayrshire, 2.9.13. Died: Liverpool, 29.9.81.
**Playing career:**

Carlisle United: 1932-1933, 16 League appearances, 0 goals. Preston North End: 1933-1949, 297 League appearances, 13 goals, FA Cup winner's medal 1937/38, FA Cup loser's medal 1936/37, Promotion from Second Division 1933/34. 5 Scotland caps 1938-1939. 7 wartime internationals.

**Management career**

Carlisle United, March 1949 - July 1951, best position third in Division 3 North 1950/51. Grimsby Town, July 1951 - January 1954, best position 2nd in Division 3 North 1951/52. Workington Town, January 1954 - November 1955, best position 8th in Division 3 North in 1954/55. Huddersfield Town, assistant manager December 1955, then manager November 1956 - November 1959, best position 12th in Division 2 1956/57 (6th in Division 2 in 1959/60, having resigned in December). Liverpool, December 1959 - July 1974. Honours: League Champions 1963/64, 1965/66, 1972/73, runners-up 1968/69, 1973/74; Second Division Champions 1961/62; FA Cup winners 1964/65, finalists 1970/71; UEFA Cup winners 1972/73; European Cup Winners' Cup finalists 1965/66, semi-finalists 1970/71; European Cup semi-finalists 1964/65.

**BOB PAISLEY** Born: Hetton-le-Hole, County Durham, 23.1.19.
**Playing career**

Bishop Auckland (amateur) 1938-1939, FA Amateur Cup winner's medal 1938/39. Liverpool 1939-1954, 253 League appearances, 10 goals, League Championship medal 1946/47.

**Management and coaching career**

Liverpool, assistant trainer 1954, chief trainer 1959, manager July 1974 - June 1983. Honours: European Cup winners 1976/77, 1977/78, 1980/81; UEFA Cup winners 1975/76; League Champions 1975/76, 1976/77, 1978/79, 1979/80, 1981/82, 1982/83, runners-up 1974/75, 1977/78; League Cup winners 1980/81, 1981/82, 1982/83, finalists 1977/78; FA Cup finalists 1976/77.

**JOE FAGAN** Born: Liverpool, 12.3.21.
**Playing career**

Manchester City 1938-1951, 148 League appearances, 2 goals, Division Two Championship medal 1946/47. Nelson (non-League, player-manager) 1951-1953. Bradford Park Avenue 1953, 3 League appearances, 0 goals.

**Management and coaching career**

Rochdale, trainer 1953-1958. Liverpool, reserve-team trainer 1958, first-team trainer 1966, assistant manager 1979, manager June 1983 - May 1985. Honours: European Cup winners 1983/84, finalists 1984/85; League Champions 1983/84, runners-up 1984/85; League Cup winners 1983/84.

**KENNY DALGLISH** Born: Glasgow, 4.3.51.
**Playing career**

Celtic 1967-1977, 204 League appearances (4 as substitute), 112 goals, Scottish

Championship medals 1971/72, 1972/73, 1973/74, 1975/76, 1976/77; Scottish Cup winner's medals 1971/72, 1973/74, 1974/75, 1976/77; Scottish League Cup winner's medal 1974/75. Liverpool 1977-1991, 358 League appearances (16 as substitute), 118 goals; European Cup winner's medals 1977/78, 1980/81, 1983/84; League Championship medals 1978/79, 1979/80, 1981/82, 1982/83, 1983/84, 1985/86 (as player-manager); FA Cup winner's medal 1985/86 (as player-manager); League Cup winner's medals 1980/81, 1981/82, 1982/83, 1983/84. 102 Scotland caps 1971-1986.

**Management career**

Liverpool June 1985 - February 1991. Honours: League Champions 1985/86, 1987/88, 1989/90, runners-up 1986/87, 1988/89; FA Cup winners 1985/86, 1988/89, finalists 1987/88; League Cup finalists 1986/87. Blackburn Rovers, October 1991 onwards, Promotion to Premier League in 1991/92, best position 2nd in Premiership 1993/94.


# RONNIE MORAN Born: Liverpool, 28.2.34.

**Playing career**

Liverpool 1952-1967, 343 League appearances, 14 goals; League Championship medal 1963/64; Second Division Championship medal 1961/62.

**Management and coaching career**

Liverpool, youth-team trainer 1966, reserve-team trainer 1971, first-team coach 1974, caretaker manager February 1991 - April 1991 and January 1994.


# GRAEME SOUNESS Born: Edinburgh, 6.5.53.

**Playing career**

Tottenham Hotspur 1969-1973, no League appearances. Middlesbrough 1973-1978, 176 League appearances (2 as substitute), 22 goals, Second Division Championship medal 1973/74. Liverpool 1978-1984, 247 appearances (1 as substitute), 38 goals; European Cup winner's medals 1977/78, 1980/81, 1983/84; League Championship medals 1978/79, 1979/80, 1981/82, 1982/83, 1983/84; League Cup winner's medals 1980/81, 1981/82, 1982/83, 1983/84. Sampdoria of Italy 1984-1986, 56 League appearances, 8 goals. Glasgow Rangers 1986-1990, 50 League appearances (12 as substitute), 3 goals; Scottish Championship medal 1986/87; Scottish Cup loser's medal 1988/89. 54 Scotland caps 1975-1986.

**Management career**

Glasgow Rangers May 1986 - April 1991. Honours: Scottish Champions 1986/87, 1988/89, 1989/90, 1990/91 (left in April); Scottish Cup finalists 1988/89; Scottish League Cup winners 1986/87, 1987/88, 1988/89, 1990/91. Liverpool April 1991 - January 1994. Honours: FA Cup winners 1991/92, best League position 6th in First Division 1991/92 and 6th in Premier League 1992/93.


# ROY EVANS Born: Bootle, Liverpool, 4.10.48.

**Playing career**

Liverpool 1964-1974, 9 League appearances, 0 goals.

**Management and coaching career:**

Reserve-team trainer 1974, first-team trainer 1983, assistant manager 1993, manager February 1994 onwards.

# BOUNTY OF THE BOOT ROOM

*Liverpool's record in senior competition since Bill Shankly arrived at Anfield.*

**1959/60**   3rd in Div 2; FA Cup - beat Leyton Orient, lost to Manchester United in 4th rd.

**1960/61**   3rd in Div 2; FA Cup - beat Coventry City, lost to Sunderland in 4th rd; League Cup - beat Luton Town, lost to Southampton in 3rd rd.

**1961/62**   1st in Div 2; FA Cup - beat Chelsea and Oldham Athletic, lost to Preston North End in 5th rd second replay.

**1962/63**   8th in Div 1; FA Cup - beat Wrexham, Burnley, Arsenal and West Ham United, lost to Leicester City in semi-final.

**1963/64**   1st in Div 1; FA Cup - beat Derby County, Port Vale and Arsenal, lost to Swansea Town in quarter-final.

**1964/65**   7th in Div 1; FA Cup Winners - beat West Bromwich Albion, Stockport County, Bolton Wanderers, Leicester City, Chelsea, and Leeds United in final; European Cup - beat Reykjavik, Anderlecht and FC Cologne, lost to Inter Milan in semi-final.

**1965/66**   1st in Div 1; FA Cup - lost to Chelsea in 3rd rd; European Cup Winners' Cup - beat Juventus, Standard Liege, Honved and Celtic, lost to Borussia Dortmund in final.

**1966/67**   5th in Div 1; FA Cup - beat Watford and Aston Villa, lost to Everton in 5th rd; European Cup - beat Petrolul Ploesti, lost to Ajax in 1st rd proper.

**1967/68**   3rd in Div 1; FA Cup - beat Bournemouth, Walsall and Tottenham Hotspur, lost to West Bromwich Albion in quarter-final second replay; League Cup - lost to Bolton in 2nd rd replay; European Fairs Cup - beat Malmo and TSV Munich, lost to Ferencvaros in 3rd rd.

**1968/69**   2nd in Div 1; FA Cup - beat Doncaster Rovers and Burnley, lost to Leicester City in 5th rd replay; League Cup - beat Sheffield United and Swansea Town, lost to Arsenal in 4th rd; European Fairs Cup - lost to Atletico Bilbao in 1st rd.

**1969/70**   5th in Div 1; FA Cup - beat Coventry City, Wrexham and Leicester City, lost to Watford in quarter-final; League Cup - beat Watford, lost to Manchester City in 3rd rd; European Fairs Cup - beat Dundalk, lost to Vitoria Setubal.

**1970/71**   5th in Div 1; FA Cup - beat Aldershot, Swansea City, Southampton, Tottenham Hotspur and Everton, lost to Arsenal in final; League Cup - beat Mansfield Town, lost to Swindon Town in 3rd rd; European Fairs Cup - beat Ferencvaros, Dynamo Bucharest, Hibernian and Bayern Munich, lost to Leeds United in semi-final.

**1971/72**   3rd in Div 1; FA Cup - beat Oxford United, lost to Leeds United in 4th rd replay; League Cup - beat Hull City and Southampton, lost to West Ham United in 4th rd; European Cup Winners' Cup - beat Servette Geneva, lost to Bayern Munich in 2nd rd.

**1972/73**   1st in Div 1; FA Cup - beat Burnley, lost to Manchester City in 4th rd replay; League Cup - beat Carlisle United, West Bromwich Albion and Leeds United, lost to Tottenham

Hotspur in quarter-final replay; UEFA Cup Winners - beat Eintracht Frankfurt, AEK Athens, Dynamo Berlin, Dynamo Dresden, Tottenham Hotspur, and Borussia Moenchengladbach in final.

**1973/74**   2nd in Div 1; FA Cup Winners - beat Doncaster Rovers, Carlisle United, Ipswich Town, Bristol City, Leicester City, and Newcastle United in final; League Cup - beat West Ham United, Sunderland and Hull City, lost to Wolverhampton Wanderers in quarter-final; European Cup - beat Jeunesse D'Esch, lost to Red Star Belgrade in 2nd rd.

**1974/75**   2nd in Div 1; FA Cup - beat Stoke City, lost to Ipswich Town in 4th rd; League Cup - beat Brentford and Bristol City, lost to Middlesbrough in 4th rd; European Cup Winners' Cup - beat Stromgodset Drammen, lost to Ferencvaros.

**1975/76**   1st in Div 1; FA Cup - beat West Ham United, lost to Derby County in 4th rd; League Cup - beat York City, lost to Burnley in 3rd rd replay; UEFA Cup Winners - beat Hibernian, Real Sociedad, Slask Wroclaw, Dynamo Dresden, Barcelona, and FC Bruges in final.

**1976/77**   1st in Div 1; FA Cup - beat Crystal Palace, Carlisle United, Oldham Athletic, Middlesbrough and Everton, lost to Manchester United in final; League Cup - lost to West Bromwich Albion in 2nd rd; European Cup Winners - beat Crusaders, Trabzonspor, St Etienne, FC Zurich, and Borussia Moenchengladbach in final.

**1977/78**   2nd in Div 1; FA Cup - lost to Chelsea in 3rd rd; League Cup - beat Chelsea, Derby County, Coventry City, Wrexham and Arsenal, lost to Nottingham Forest in final replay; European Cup Winners - beat Dynamo Dresden, Benfica, Borussia Moenchengladbach, and FC Bruges in final.

**1978/79**   1st in Div 1; FA Cup - beat Southend United, Blackburn Rovers, Burnley and Ipswich Town, lost to Manchester United in semi-final; League Cup - lost to Sheffield United in 2nd rd; European Cup - lost to Nottingham Forest in 1st rd.

**1979/80**   1st in Div 1; FA Cup - beat Grimsby Town, Nottingham Forest, Bury and Tottenham Hotspur, lost to Arsenal in semi-final third replay; League Cup - beat Tranmere Rovers, Chesterfield, Exeter City, and Norwich City, lost to Nottingham Forest in semi-final; European Cup - lost to Dynamo Tbilisi in 1st rd.

**1980/81**   5th in Div 1; FA Cup - beat Altrincham, lost to Everton in 4th rd; League Cup Winners - beat Bradford City, Swindon Town, Portsmouth, Birmingham City, Manchester City, and West Ham United in final replay; European Cup Winners - beat Oulu Palloseura, Aberdeen, CSKA Sofia, Bayern Munich, and Real Madrid in final.

**1981/82**   1st in Div 1; FA Cup - beat Swansea City and Sunderland, lost to Chelsea in 5th rd; League Cup Winners - beat Exeter City, Middlesbrough, Arsenal, Barnsley, Ipswich Town, and Tottenham Hotspur in final; European Cup - beat Oulu Palloseura and AZ67 Alkmaar, lost to CSKA Sofia.

**1982/83**   1st in Div 1; FA Cup - beat Blackburn Rovers and Stoke City, lost to Brighton in 5th rd; League Cup Winners - beat Ipswich Town, Rotherham United, Norwich City, West Ham United, Burnley, and Manchester United in final; European Cup - beat Dundalk and JK Helsinki, lost to Widzew Lodz.

**1983/84**  1st in Div 1; FA Cup - beat Newcastle United, lost to Brighton in 4th rd; League Cup Winners - beat Brentford, Fulham, Birmingham City, Sheffield Wednesday, Walsall, and Everton in final replay; European Cup Winners - beat BK Odense, Atletico Bilbao, Benfica, Dinamo Bucharest, and AS Roma in final.

**1984/85**  2nd in Div 1; FA Cup - beat Aston Villa, Tottenham Hotspur, York City and Barnsley, lost to Manchester United in semi-final replay; League Cup - beat Stockport County, lost to Tottenham Hotspur in 3rd rd replay; European Cup - beat Lech Poznan, Benfica, Austria Vienna and Panathinaikos, lost to Juventus in final.

**1985/86**  1st in Div 1; FA Cup Winners - beat Norwich City, Chelsea, York City, Watford, Southampton, and Everton in final; League Cup - beat Oldham Athletic, Brighton, Manchester United and Ipswich Town, lost to Queen's Park Rangers in semi-final.

**1986/87**  2nd in Div 1; FA Cup - lost to Luton Town in 3rd rd second replay; League Cup - beat Fulham, Leicester City, Coventry City, Everton and Southampton, lost to Arsenal in final.

**1987/88**  1st in Div 1; FA Cup - beat Stoke City, Aston Villa, Everton, Manchester City and Nottingham Forest, lost to Wimbledon in final; League Cup - beat Blackburn Rovers, lost to Everton in 3rd rd.

**1988/89**  2nd in Div 1; FA Cup Winners - beat Carlisle United, Millwall, Hull City, Brentford, Nottingham Forest, and Everton in final; League Cup - beat Walsall and Arsenal, lost to West Ham United in 4th rd.

**1989/90**  1st in Div 1; FA Cup - beat Swansea City, Norwich City, Southampton and Queen's Park Rangers, lost to Crystal Palace in semi-final; League Cup - beat Wigan Athletic, lost to Arsenal in 3rd rd.

**1990/91**  2nd in Div 1; FA Cup - beat Blackburn Rovers and Brighton, lost to Everton in 5th rd second replay; League Cup - beat Crewe Alexandra, lost to Manchester United in 3rd rd.

**1991/92**  6th in Div 1; FA Cup Winners - beat Crewe Alexandra, Bristol Rovers, Ipswich Town, Aston Villa, Portsmouth, and Sunderland in final; League Cup - beat Stoke City and Port Vale, lost to Peterborough United in 4th rd; UEFA Cup - beat Kuusysi Lahti, Auxerre and Swarovski Tirol, lost to Genoa in 4th rd.

**1992/93**  6th in Prem; FA Cup - lost to Bolton in 3rd rd replay; League Cup - beat Chesterfield and Sheffield United, lost to Crystal Palace in 4th rd replay; European Cup Winners' Cup - beat Apollon Limassol, lost to Spartak Moscow in 2nd rd.

**1993/94**  8th in Prem; FA Cup - lost to Bristol City in 3rd rd replay; League Cup - beat Fulham and Ipswich Town, lost to Wimbledon in 4th rd replay.

# SELECTED BIBLIOGRAPHY

Liverpool In Europe by Steve Hale and Ivan Ponting, Guinness Publishing, 1992

Liverpool Player By Player by Ivan Ponting, Crowood Press, 1990

Shankly by Bill Shankly, Arthur Barker, 1976

Shankly by Phil Thompson, Bluecoat Press, 1993

Liverpool FC: Season 1959/60, edited by Eddie Marks, Marksport, 1986

Liverpool: A Complete Record by Brian Pead, Breedon Books, 1988

Bob Paisley: An Autobiography by Bob Paisley, Arthur Barker, 1983

Bob Paisley's Liverpool Scrapbook by Bob Paisley, Souvenir Press, 1979

Dalglish by Stephen Kelly, Headline Books, 1992

The FA Cup Final - A Post-War History by Ivan Ponting, TW Publications, 1993

Hunt For Goals by Roger Hunt, Pelham Books, 1969

You'll Never Walk Alone: The Official Illustrated History of Liverpool FC by Stephen Kelly, Mcdonald Queen Anne Press, 1987

Liverpool Football Club: The Inside Story by Dave Spurdens, Studio Publications, 1981

Come On The Reds by David Prole, Robert Hale, 1967

The Liverpool Football Book, edited by Ken Ashton, Stanley Paul, 1967.

Who's Who Of Liverpool by Doug Lamming, Breedon Books, 1989

Manchester City: A Complete Record by Ray Goble, Breedon Books, 1987

*On the outside looking in - the most important people of all, as Bill Shankly preached to all who would listen. They were never privileged to sit in the Boot Room, but they represent the true, living heart of Liverpool FC.*